SNAILS

ARE JUST MY SPEED!

A TOON BOOK BY
KEVIN McCLOSKEY

For Brian, my youngest brother and oldest friend.

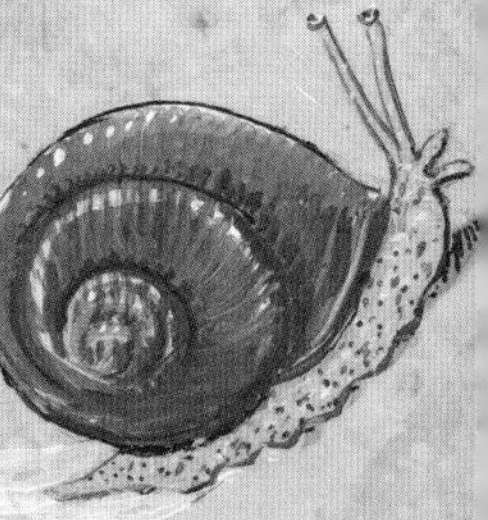

Editorial Director & Designer: FRANÇOISE MOULY

Guest Editor: RICHARD KUTNER

KEVIN McCLOSKEY'S artwork was painted with acrylic paint on parchment-style

A TOON BOOK

A TOON Book™ © 2018 Kevin McCloskey & TOON Books, an imprint of RAW Junior, LLC, 27 Greene Street, New York, NY 10013. TOON Graphics™, TOON Books®, LITTLE LIT® and TOON Into Reading!™ are trademarks of RAW Junior, LLC. All rights reserved. Medieval snails courtesy of the British Library's digitized manuscripts collection. The author found inspiration in Elisabeth Tova Bailey's book, *The Sound of a Wild Snail Eating,* and in an antique print, partially reproduced on the last pages of this book: *The Garden Snail, Helix hortensis,* from *The Naturalist's Miscellany or Coloured Figures of Natural Objects Drawn and Described Immediately from Nature,* George Shaw and Frederick P. Nodder, 1789. No part of this book may be used or reproduced in any manner whatsoever without written permission except in the case of brief quotations embodied in critical articles and reviews. All our books are Smyth Sewn (the highest library-quality binding available) and printed with soy-based inks on acid-free, woodfree paper harvested from responsible sources. Library of Congress Cataloging-in-Publication Data available upon demand. Printed in China by C&C Offset Printing Co., Ltd. Distributed to the trade by Consortium Book Sales; orders (800) 283-3572; orderentry@perseusbooks.com; www.cbsd.com.

ISBN 978-1-943145-27-0 (hardcover)

18 19 20 21 22 23 C&C 10 9 8 7 6 5 4 3 2 1

www.TOON-BOOKS.com

SNAILS LIVE IN SHELLS.

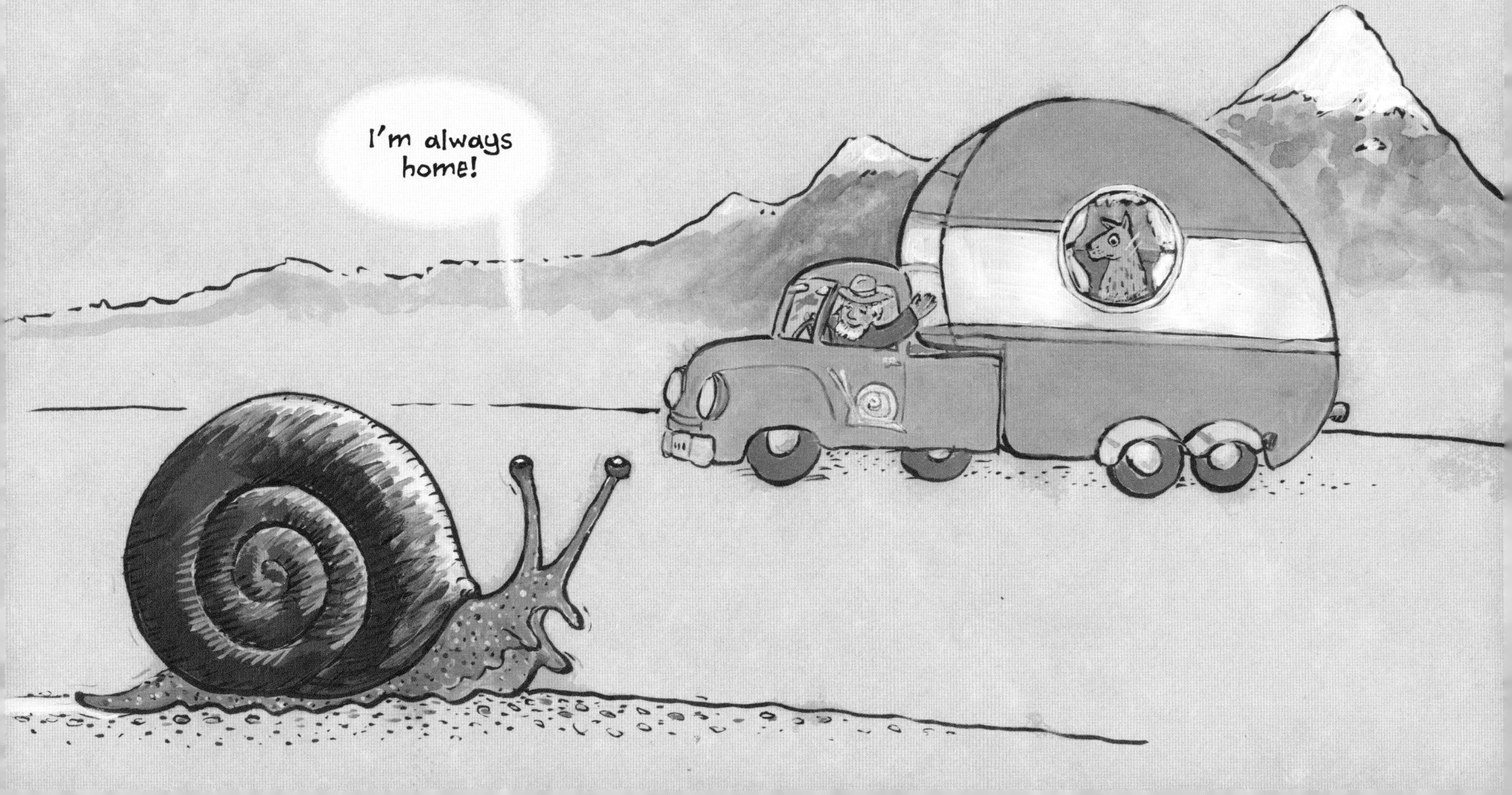
I'm always home!

THEY MOVE VERY, VERY SLOWLY...

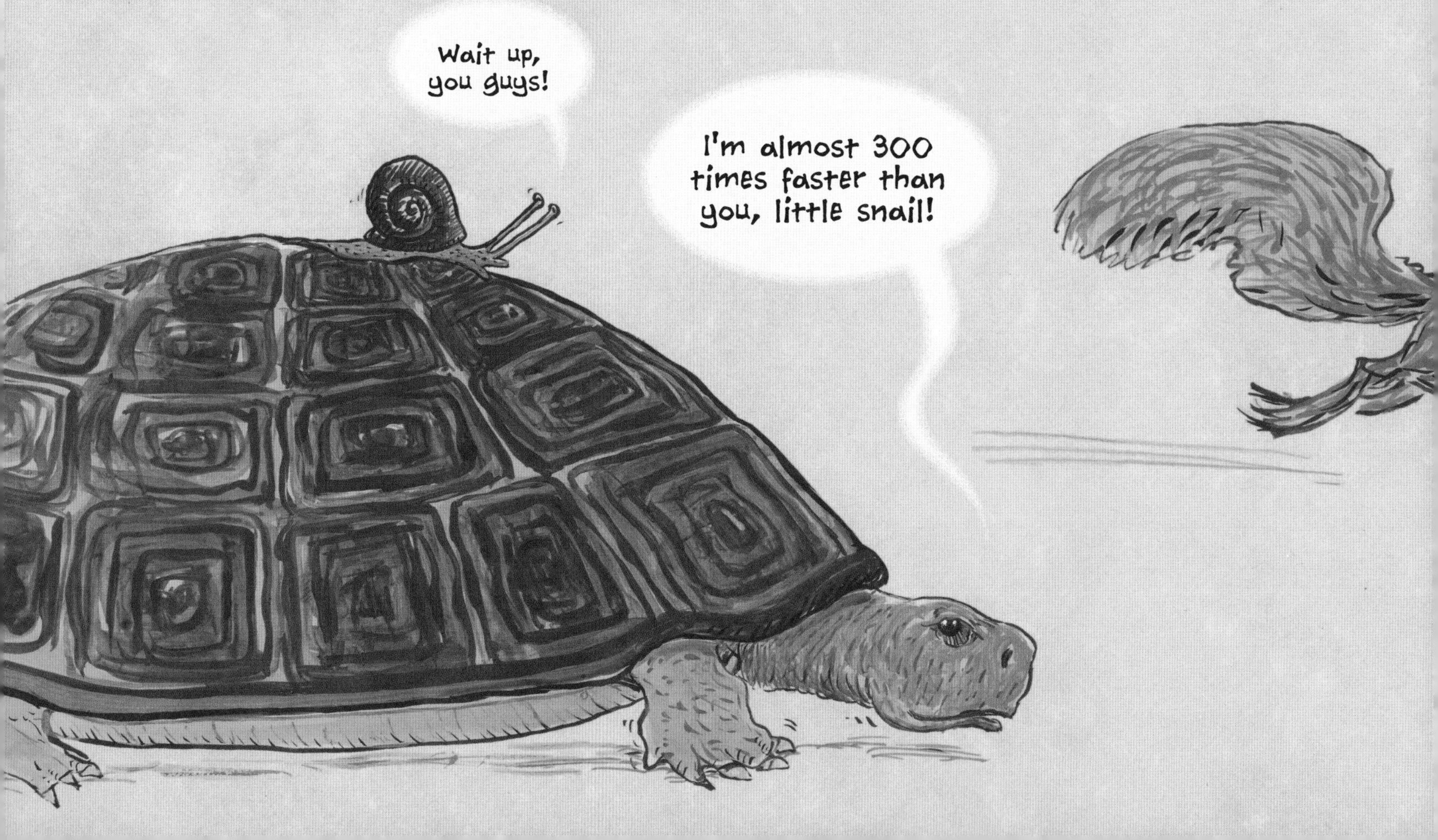
Wait up, you guys!
I'm almost 300 times faster than you, little snail!

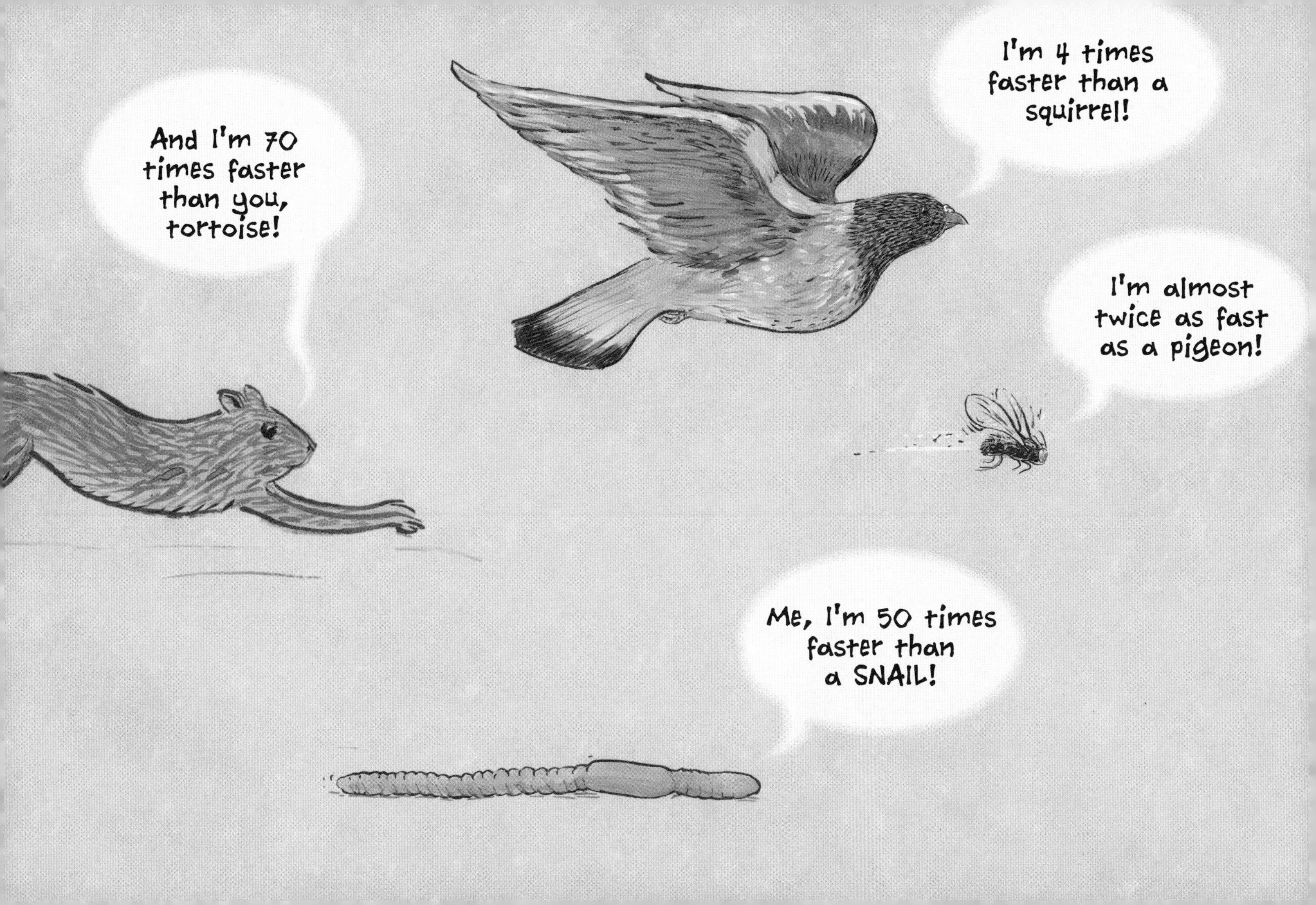
And I'm 70 times faster than you, tortoise!
I'm 4 times faster than a squirrel!
I'm almost twice as fast as a pigeon!
Me, I'm 50 times faster than a SNAIL!

IT CAN BE GOOD TO BE SLOW.
ANIMALS SEE THEIR PREY WHEN IT MOVES.

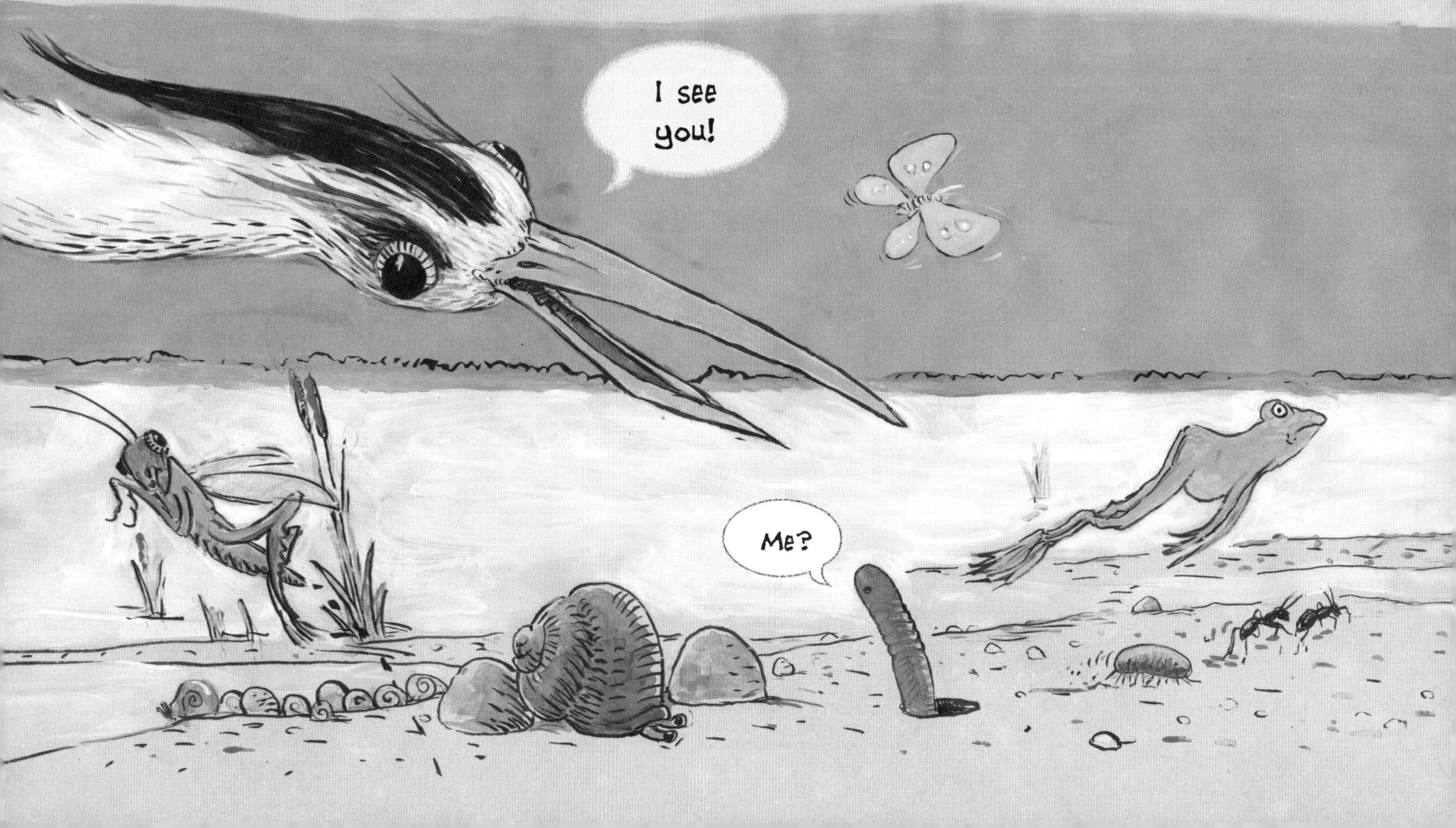
I see you!
Me?

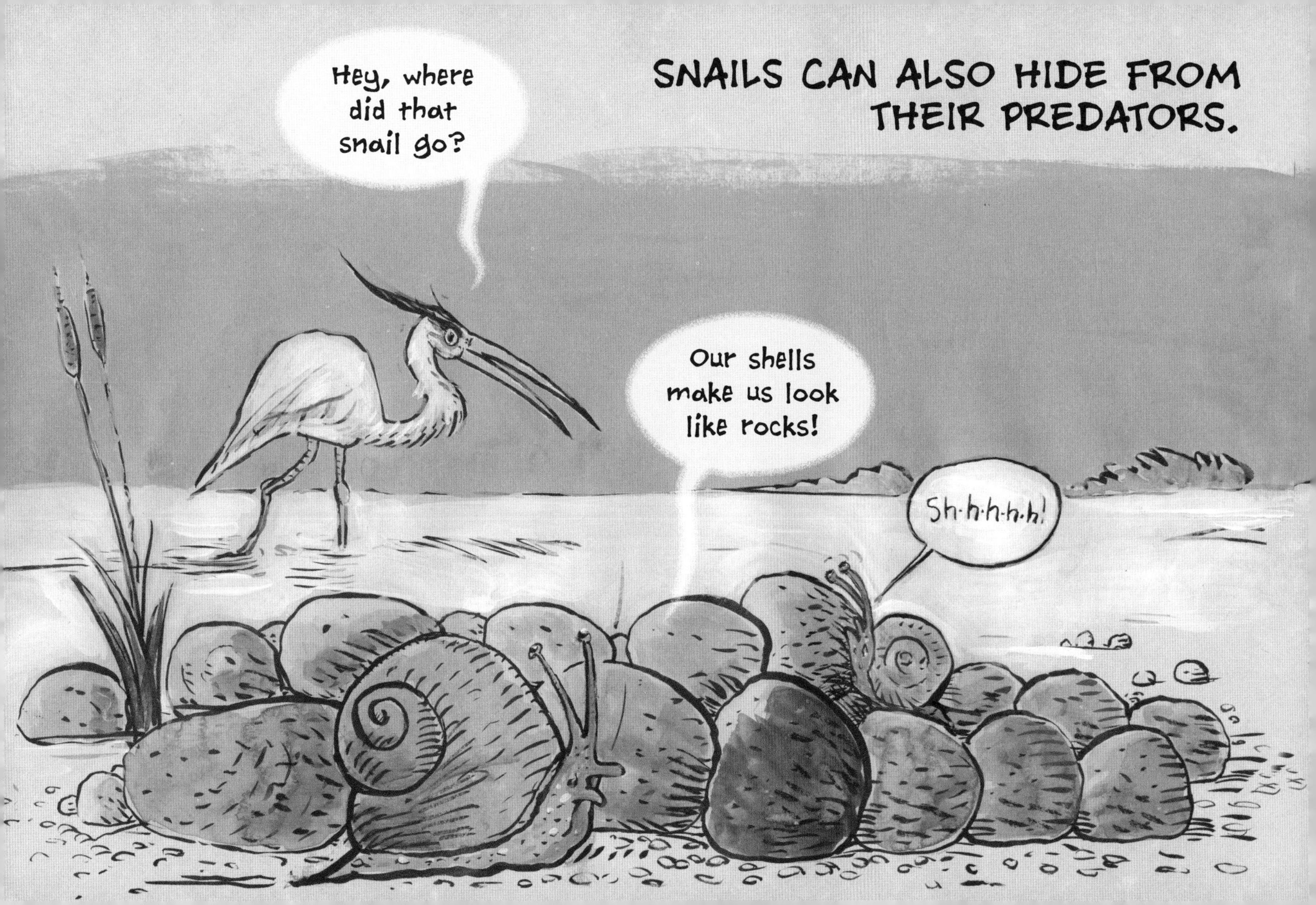
SNAILS CAN ALSO HIDE FROM THEIR PREDATORS.
Hey, where did that snail go?
Our shells make us look like rocks!
Sh-h-h-h-h!

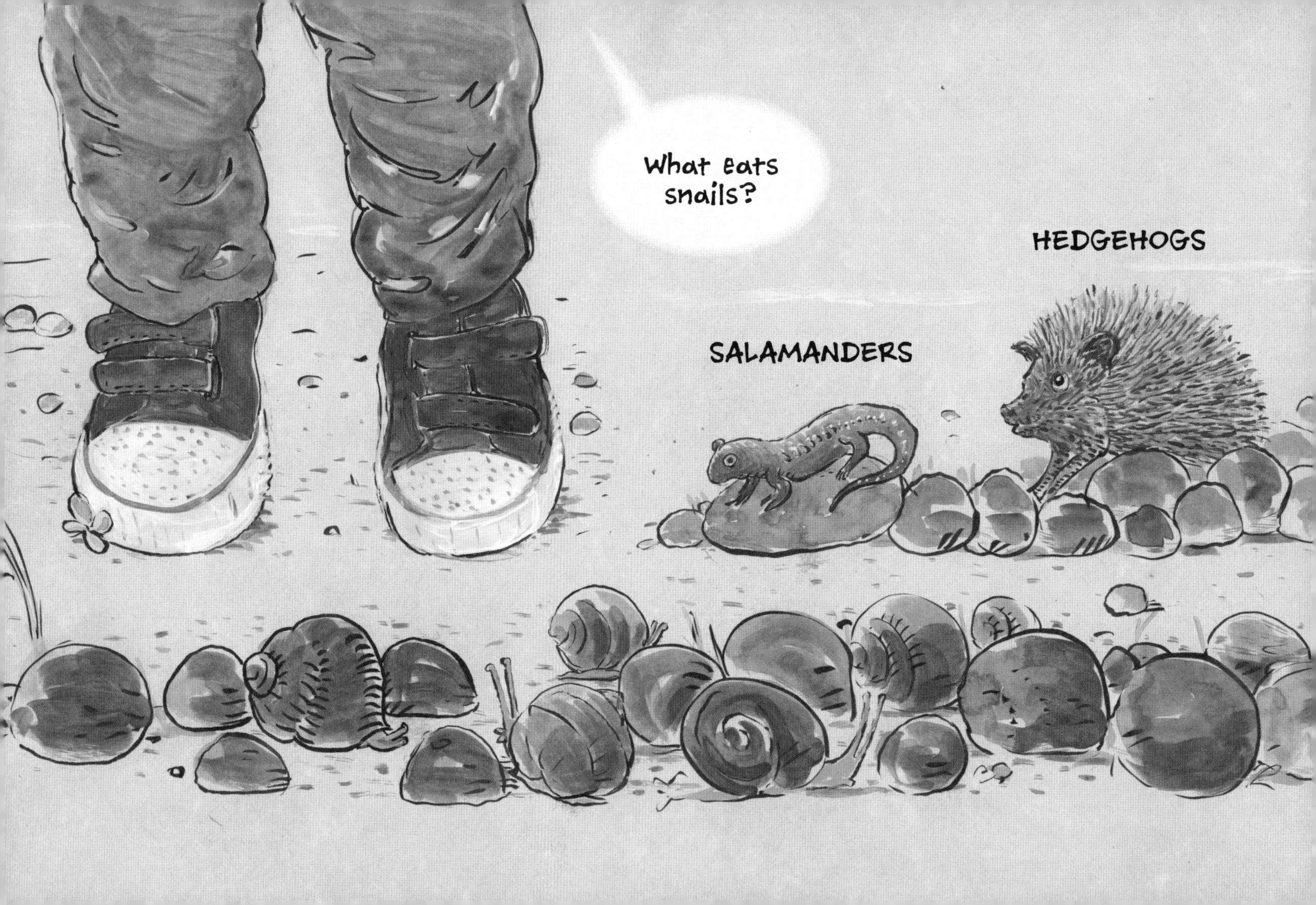
What eats snails?
HEDGEHOGS
SALAMANDERS

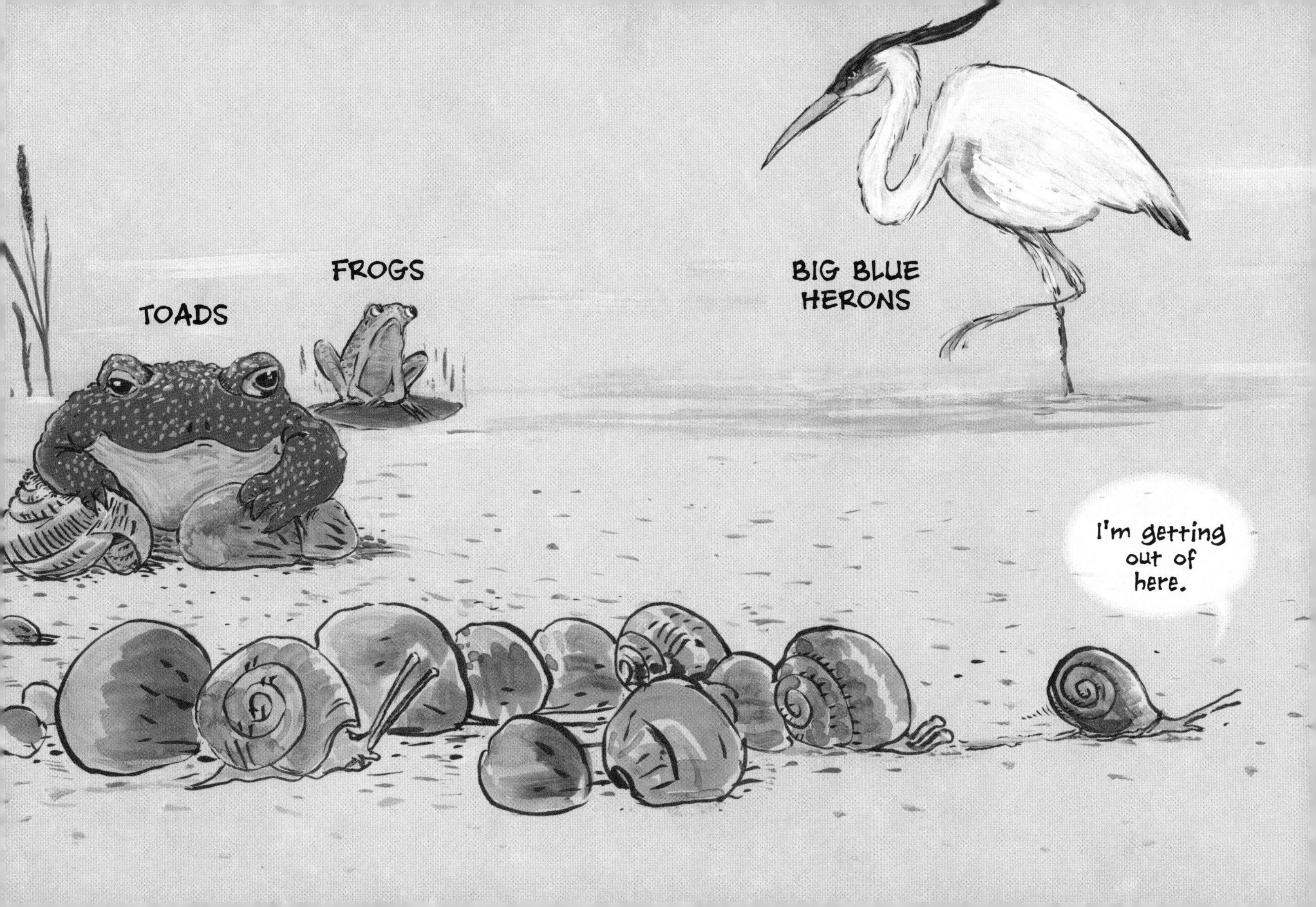
TOADS
FROGS
BIG BLUE HERONS
I'm getting out of here.

SNAILS BUILD ROADS OF SLIMY MUCUS.

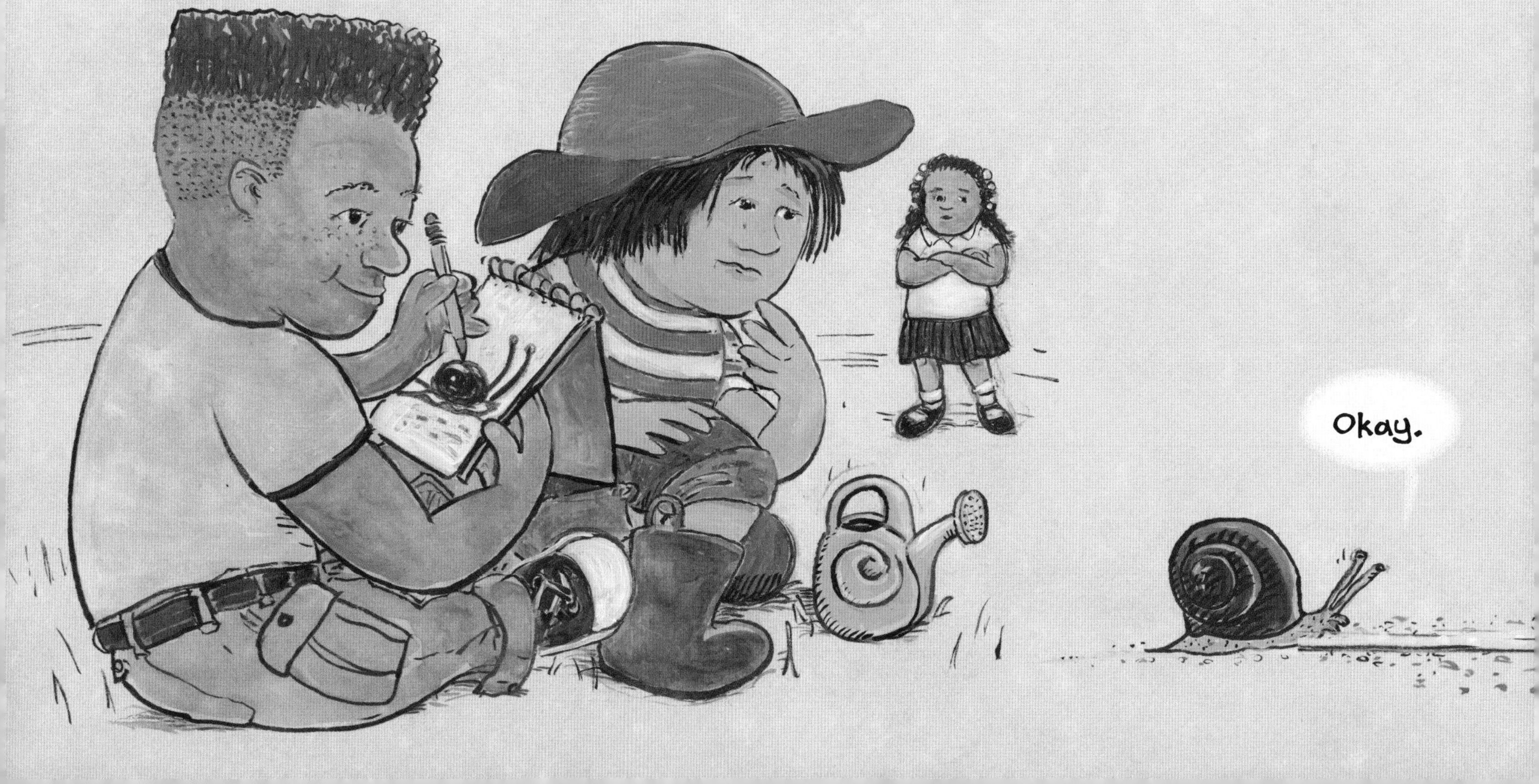
Okay.

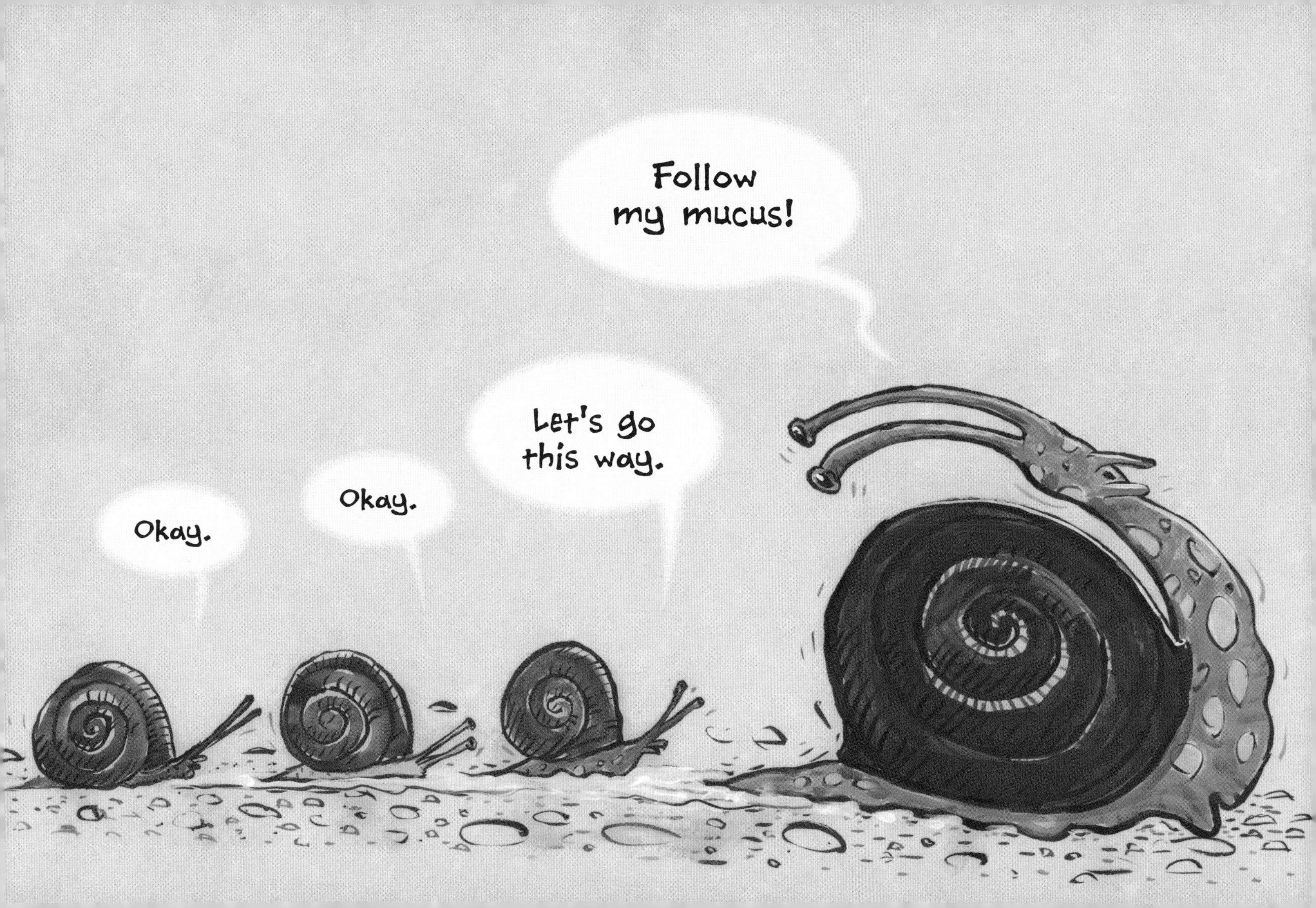
Follow my mucus!
Let's go this way.
Okay.
Okay.

THEY FOLLOW ONE ANOTHER'S TRAILS...

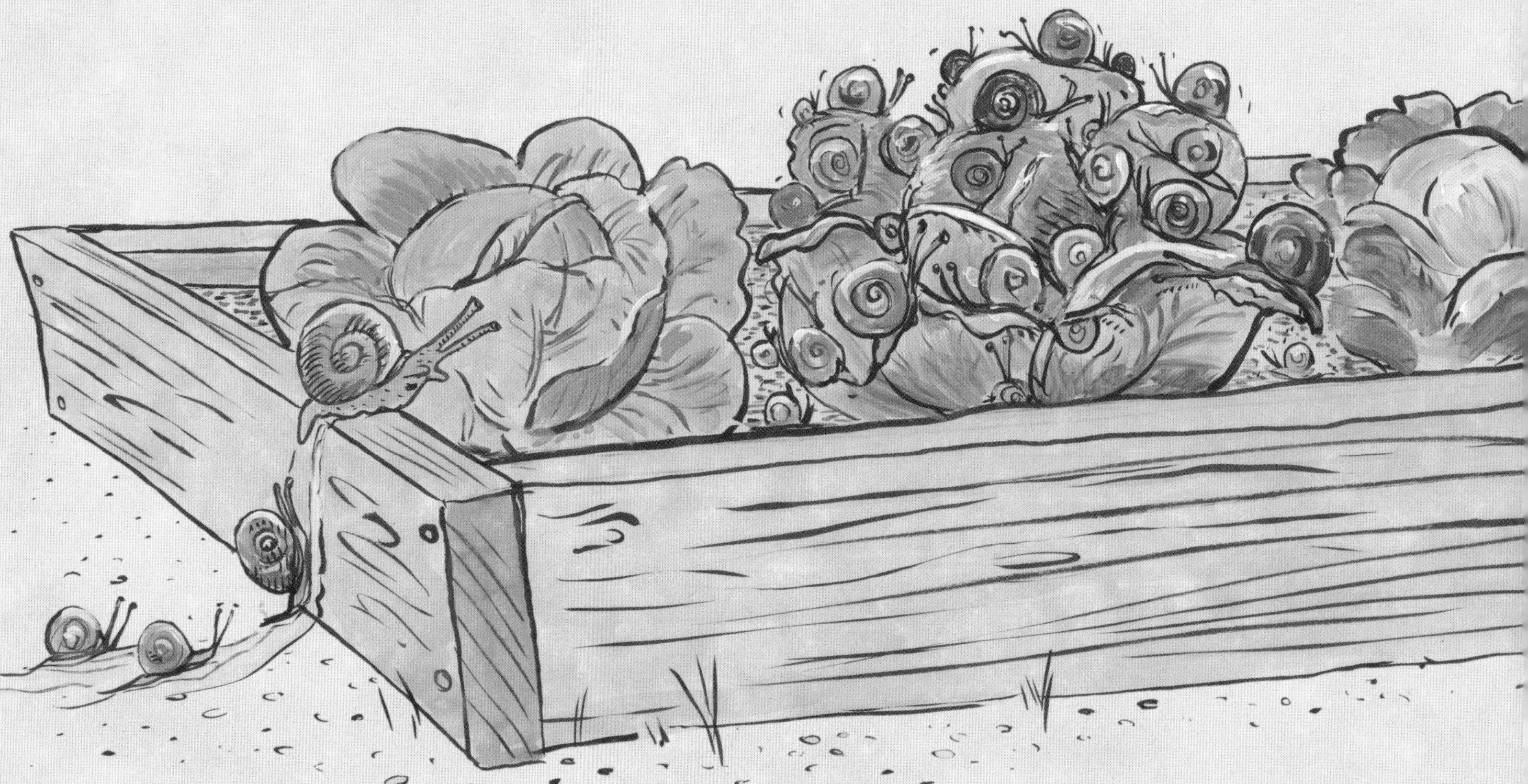

AND THEY LIKE TO EAT TOGETHER.

SNAILS MAKE A LOT OF MUCUS.

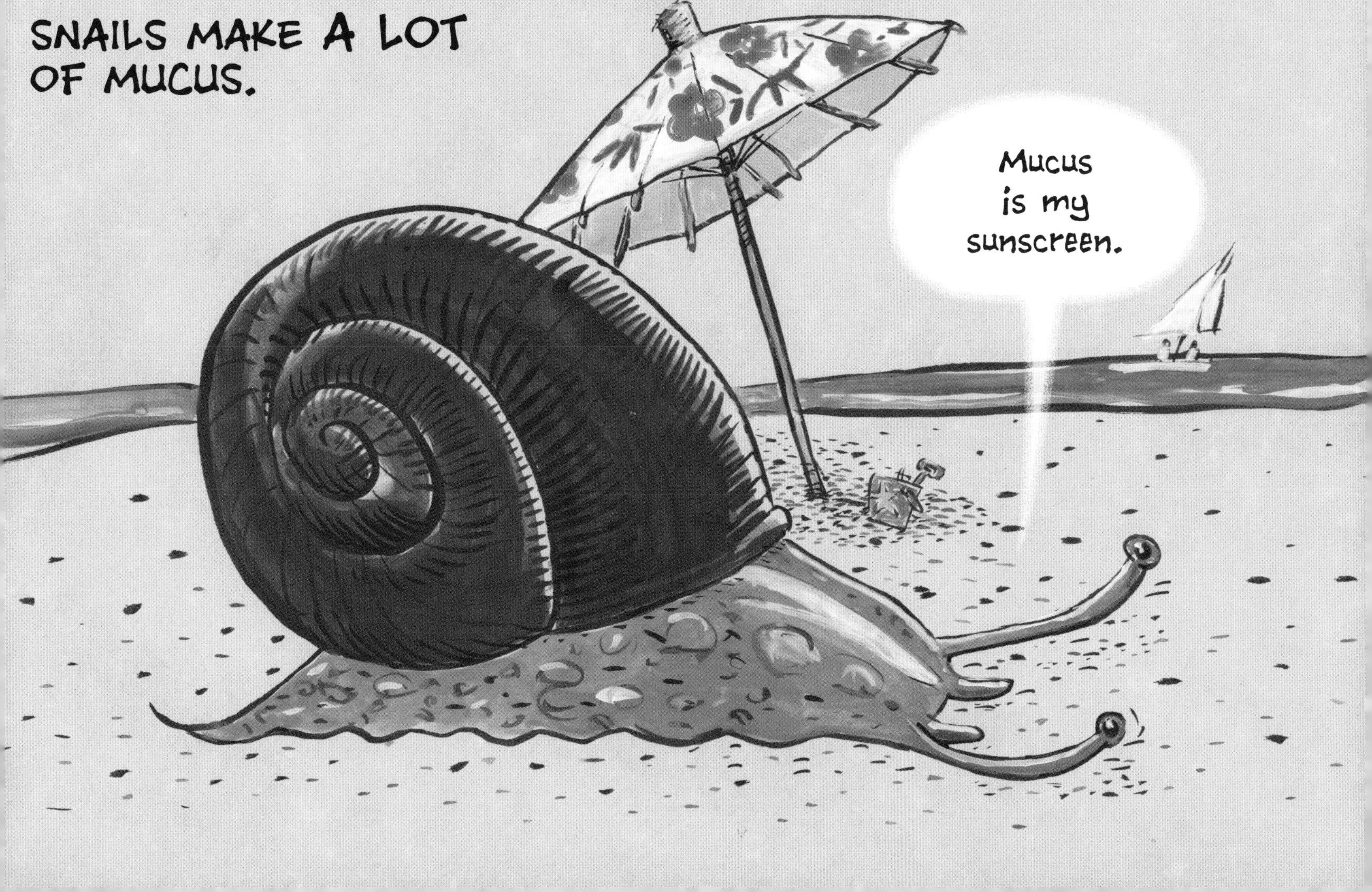
Mucus is my sunscreen.

WITH MUCUS, THEY CAN TRAVEL ON ANY SURFACE.

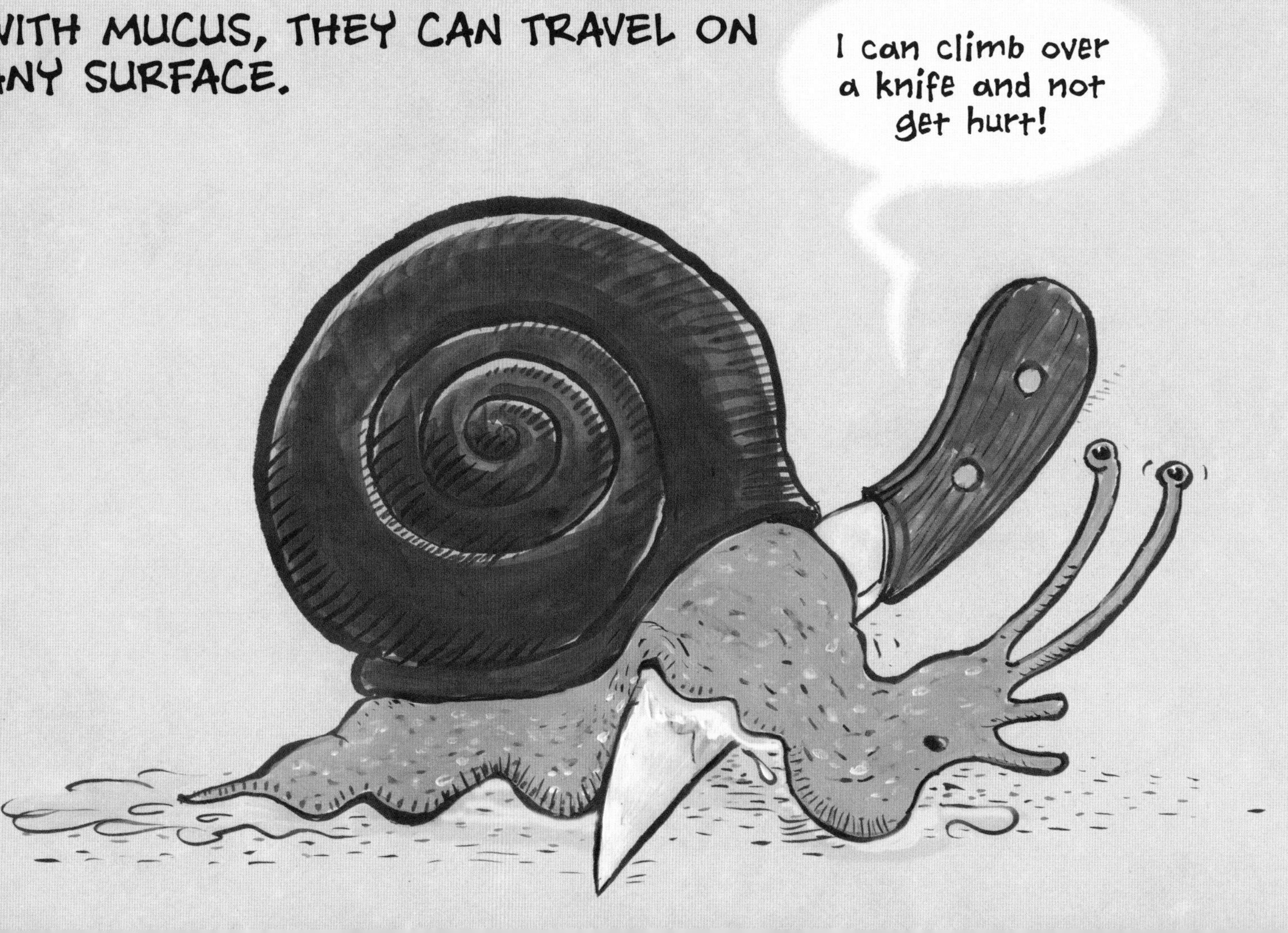
I can climb over a knife and not get hurt!

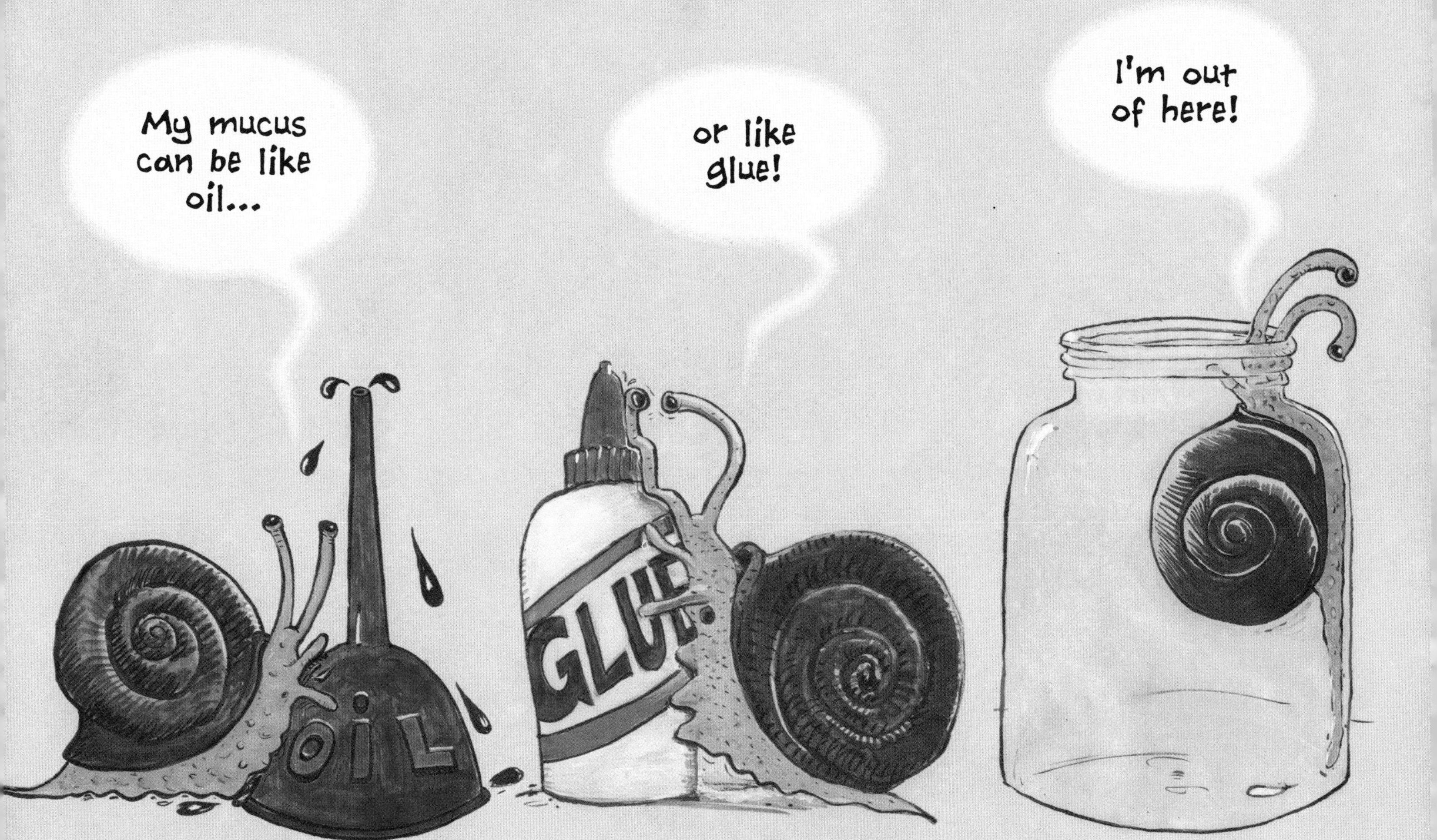
My mucus can be like oil...
or like glue!
I'm out of here!
OIL
GLUE

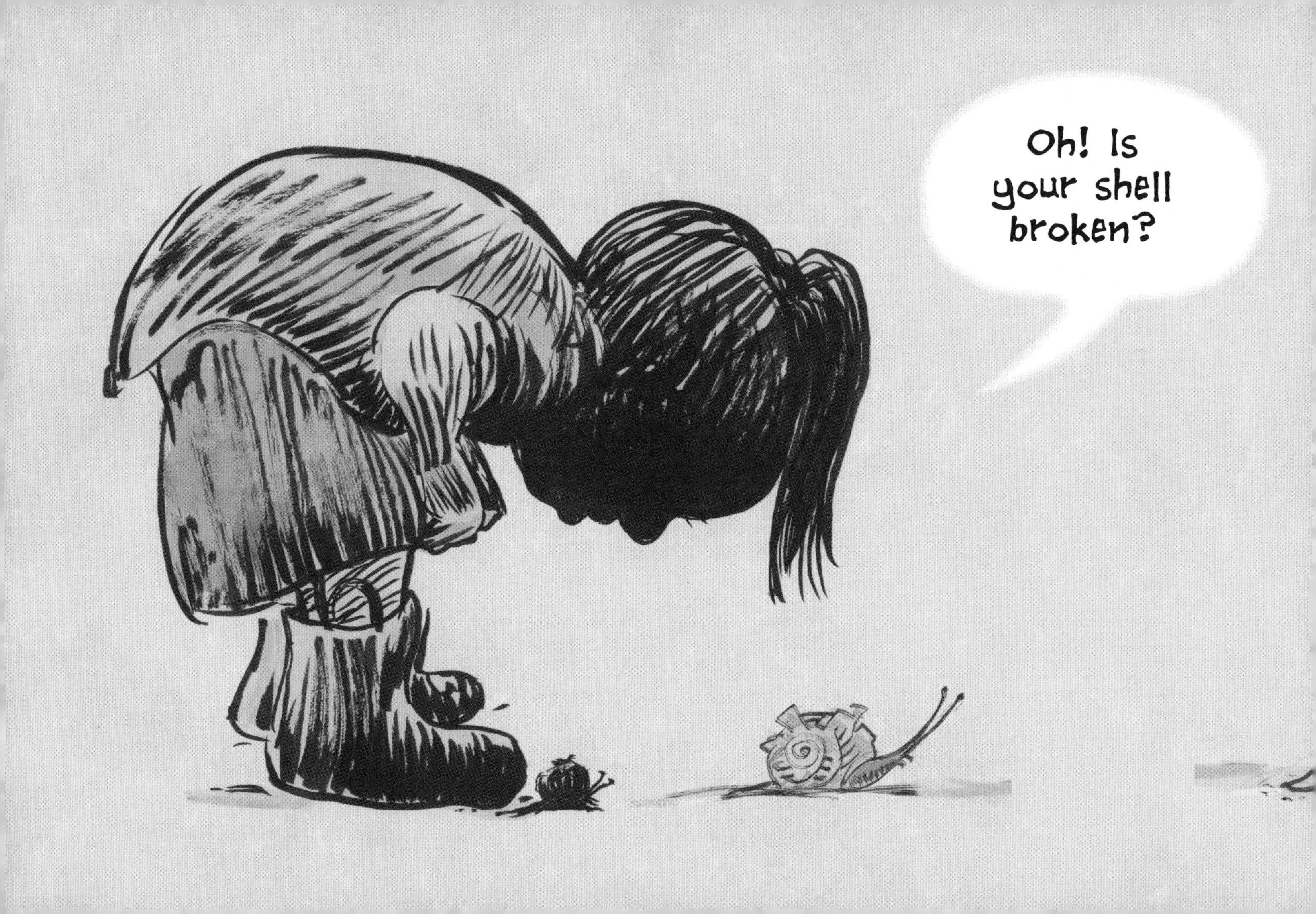
Oh! Is your shell broken?

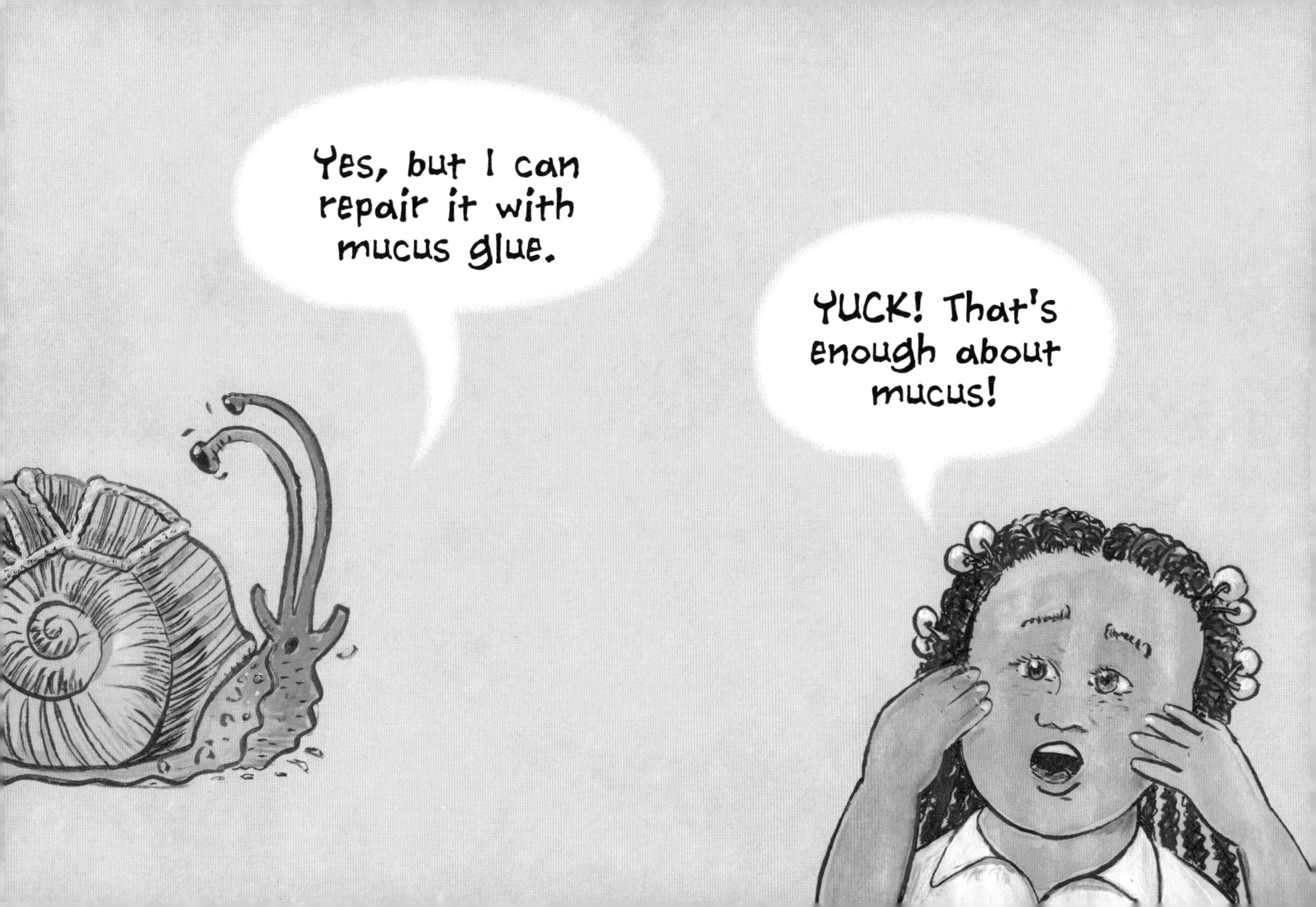
Yes, but I can repair it with mucus glue.
YUCK! That's enough about mucus!

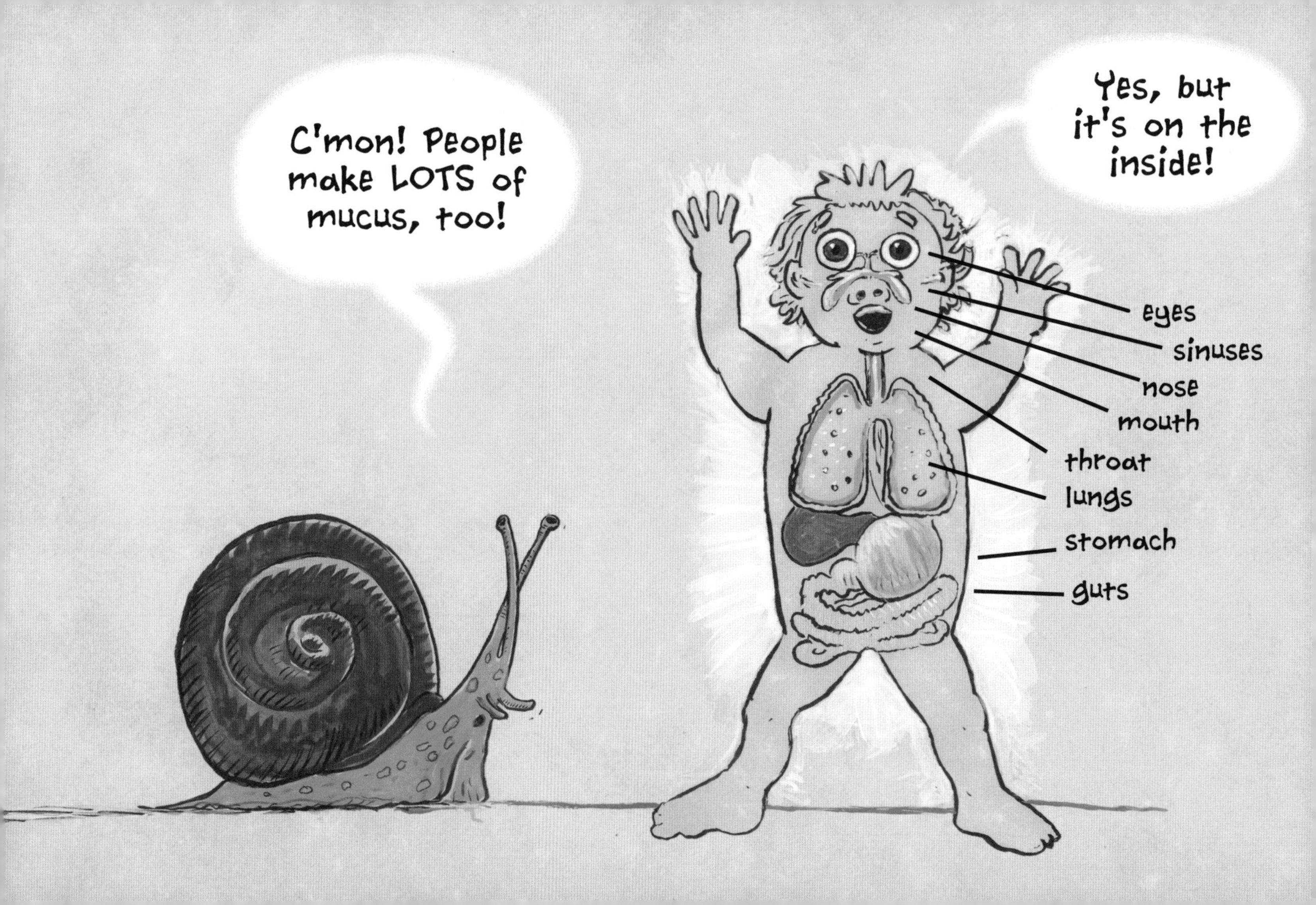
C'mon! People make LOTS of mucus, too!
Yes, but it's on the inside!
eyes
sinuses
nose
mouth
throat
lungs
stomach
guts

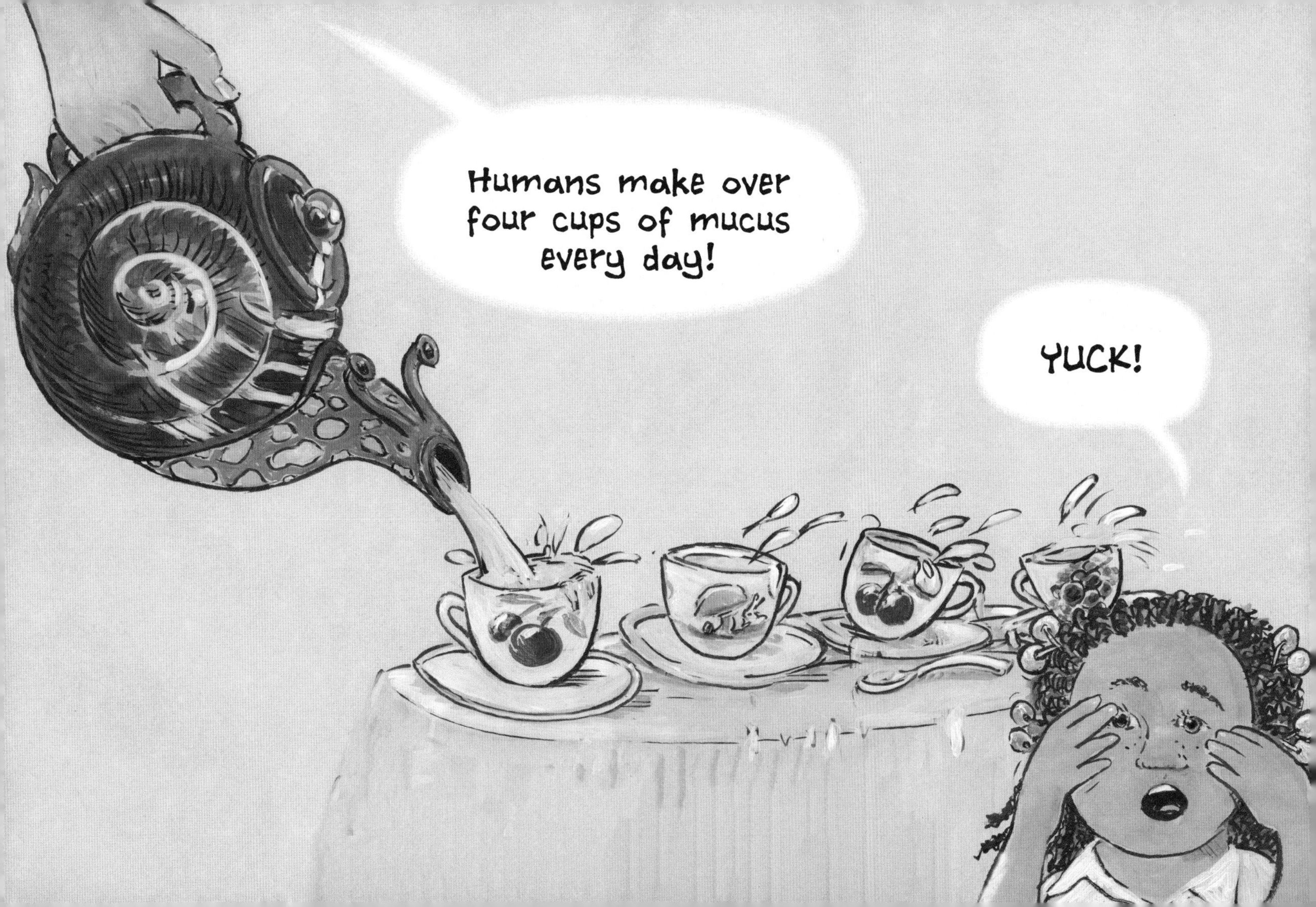
Humans make over four cups of mucus every day!
YUCK!

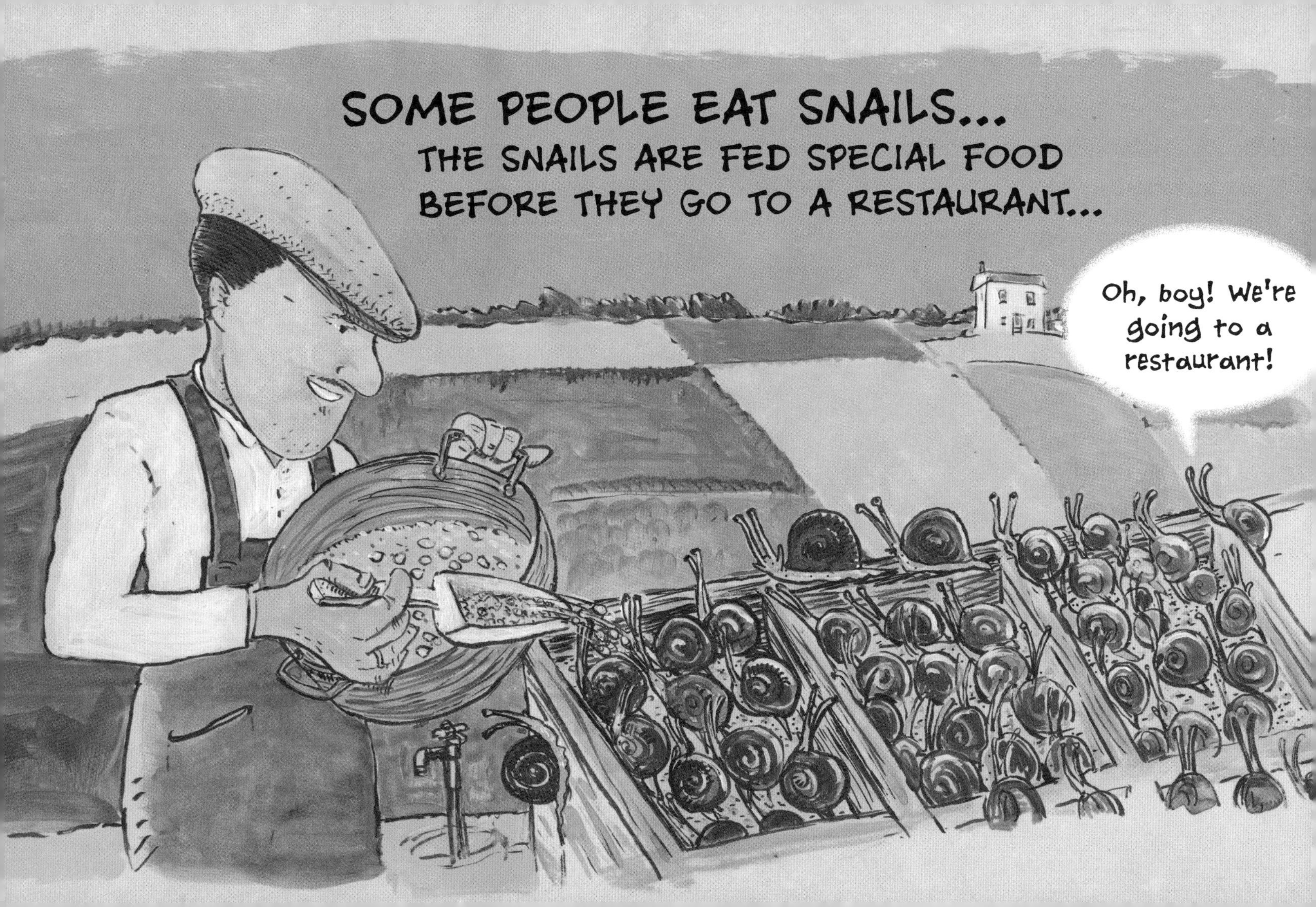
SOME PEOPLE EAT SNAILS...
THE SNAILS ARE FED SPECIAL FOOD
BEFORE THEY GO TO A RESTAURANT...
Oh, boy! We're going to a restaurant!

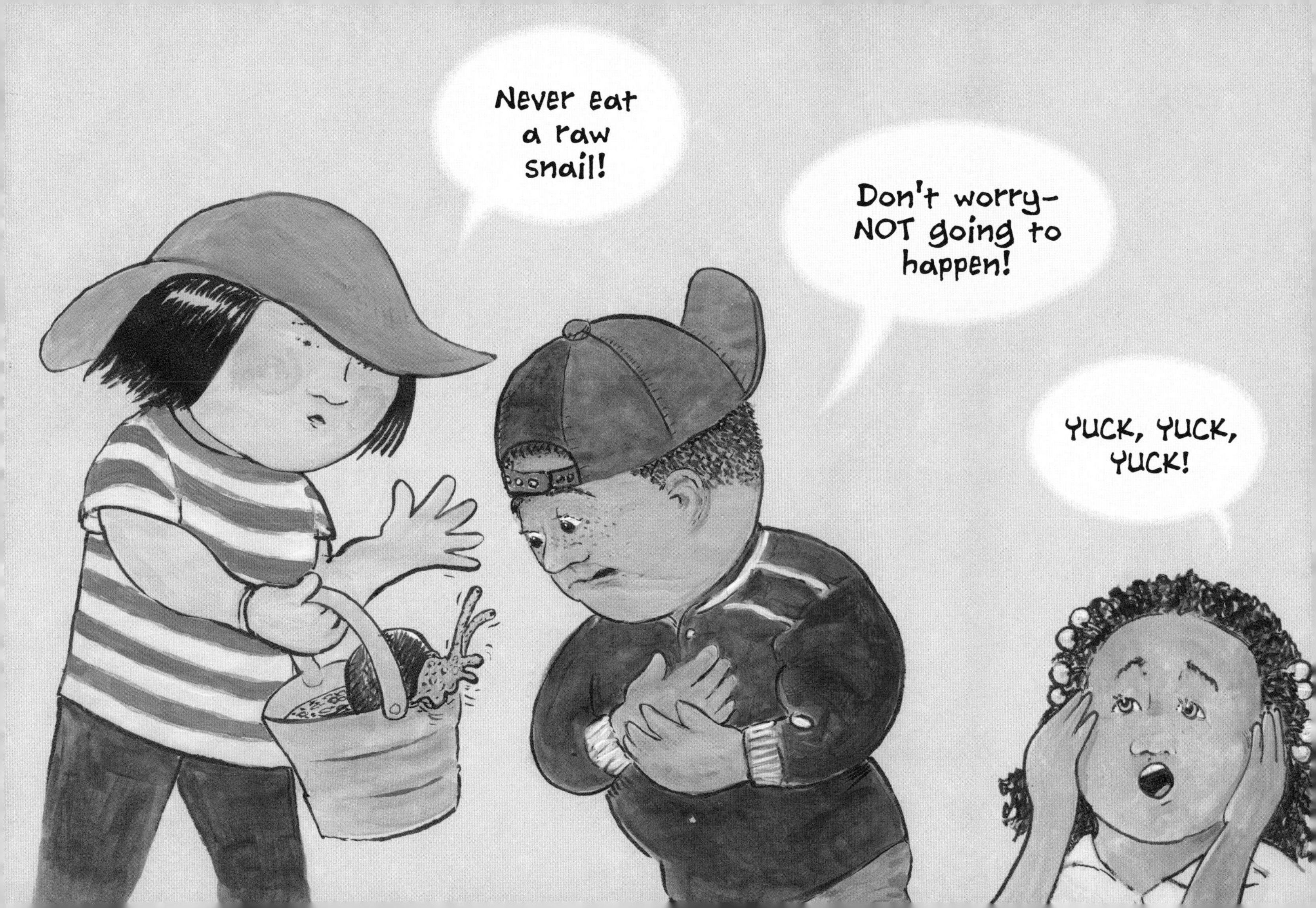
Never eat a raw snail!
Don't worry- NOT going to happen!
YUCK, YUCK, YUCK!

AMAZING SNAILS LIVE EVERYWHERE ON EARTH: AT THE BOTTOM OF THE SEA...

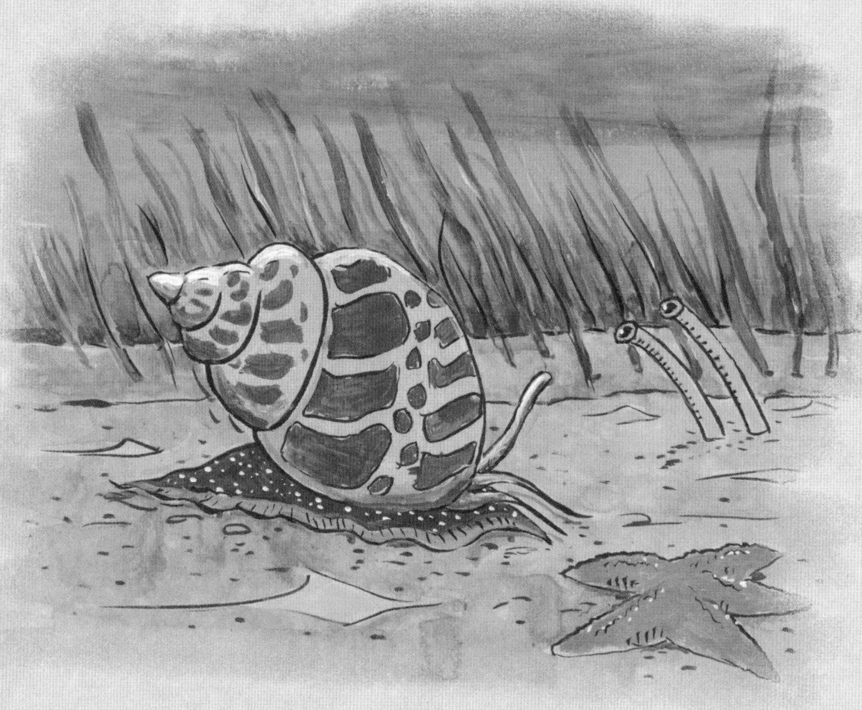

AND HIGH UP IN THE MOUNTAINS.

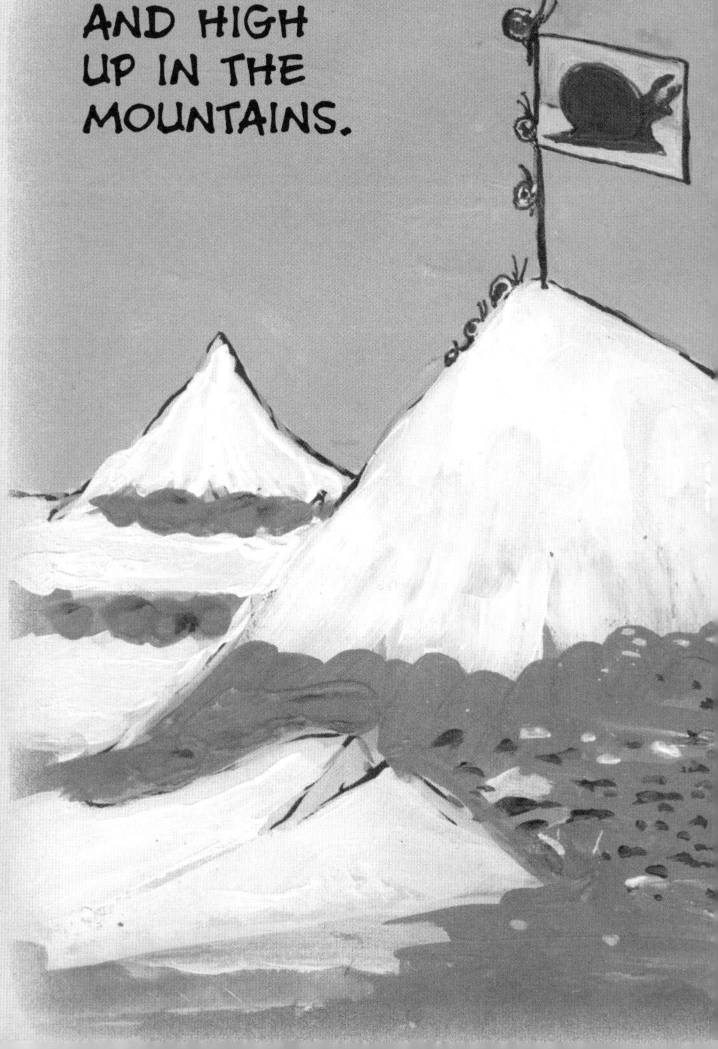

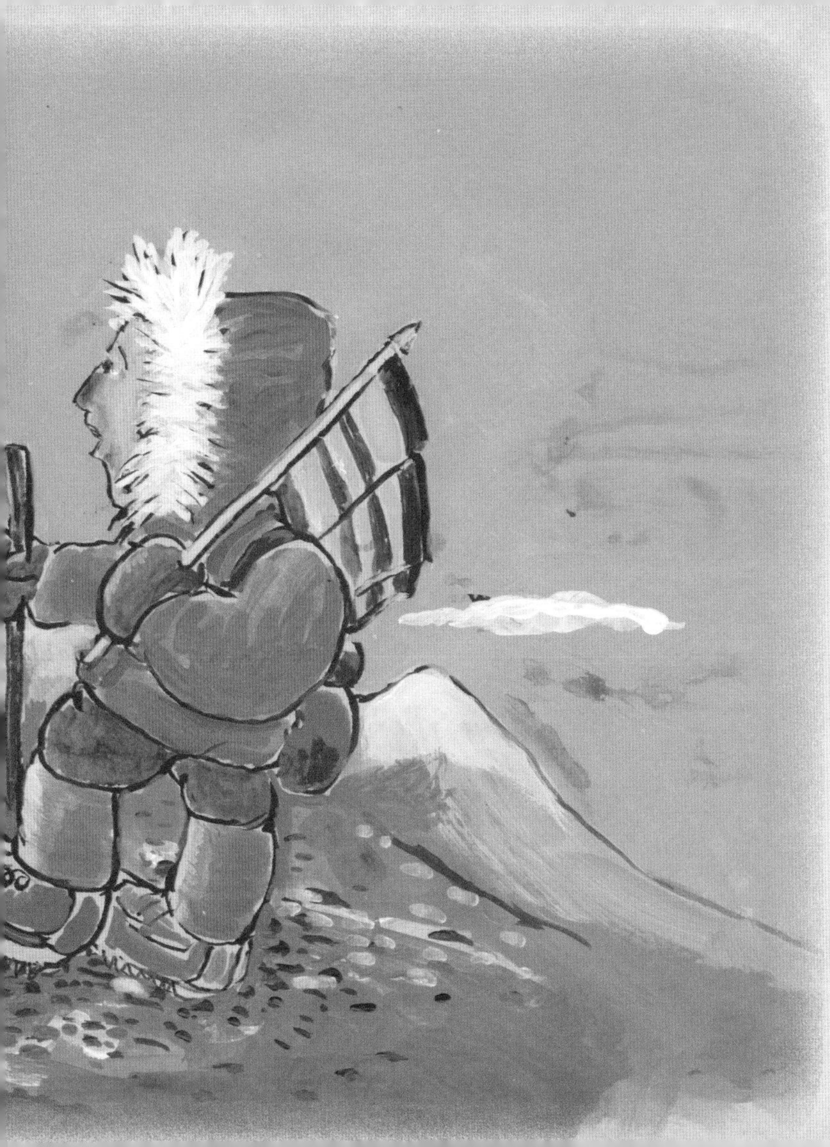

THERE ARE HAIRY SNAILS IN THE RAIN FOREST.

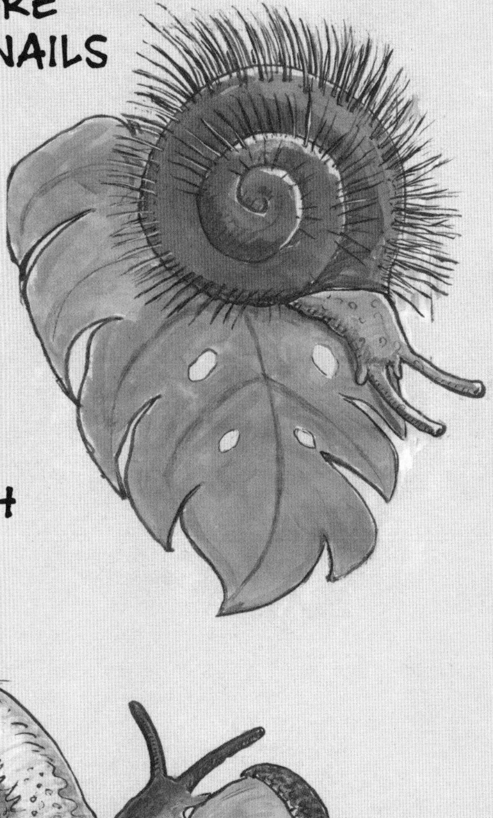

GLASS SNAILS HAVE A SEE-THROUGH SHELL.

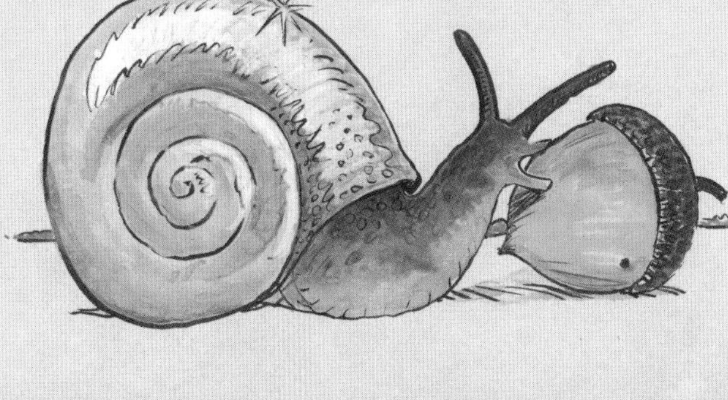

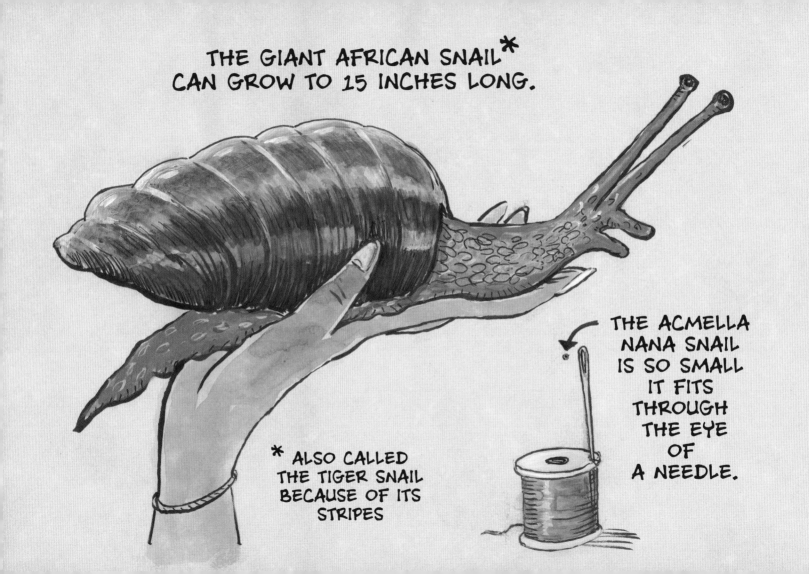

THE GIANT AFRICAN SNAIL*
CAN GROW TO 15 INCHES LONG.

* ALSO CALLED
THE TIGER SNAIL
BECAUSE OF ITS
STRIPES

THE ACMELLA
NANA SNAIL
IS SO SMALL
IT FITS
THROUGH
THE EYE
OF
A NEEDLE.

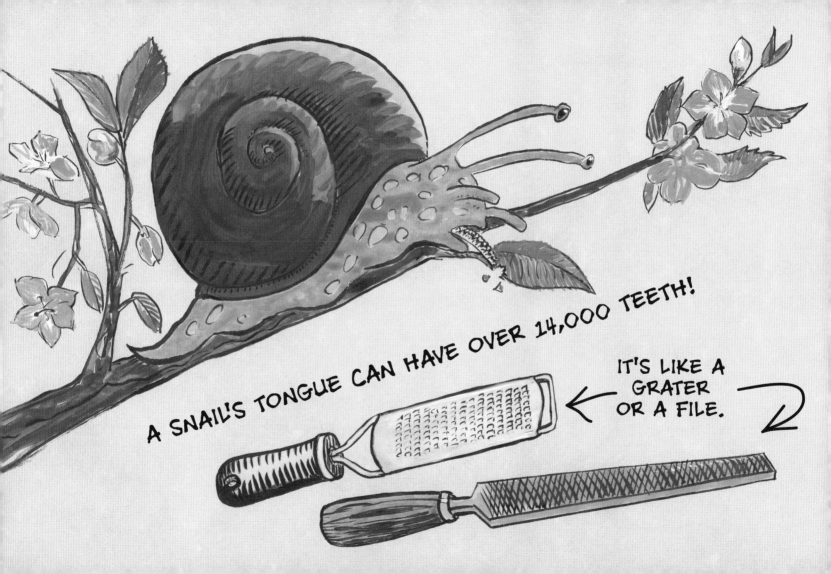

A SNAIL'S TONGUE CAN HAVE OVER 14,000 TEETH!

IT'S LIKE A GRATER OR A FILE.

EVEN THE COMMON GARDEN SNAIL IS AMAZING.

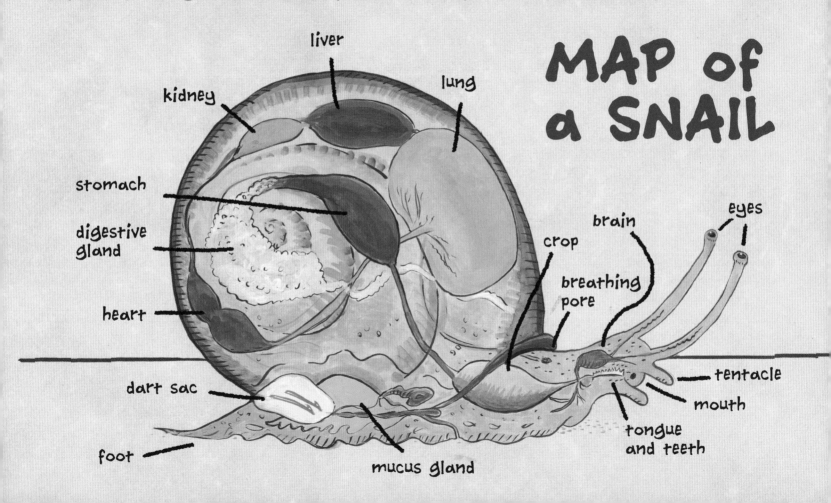

MAP of a SNAIL

liver

lung

kidney

stomach

digestive gland

heart

dart sac

foot

mucus gland

crop

brain

breathing pore

eyes

tentacle

mouth

tongue and teeth

A SNAIL'S EYES ARE WEAK, BUT IT USES ITS LOWER TENTACLES TO FEEL AND SMELL.

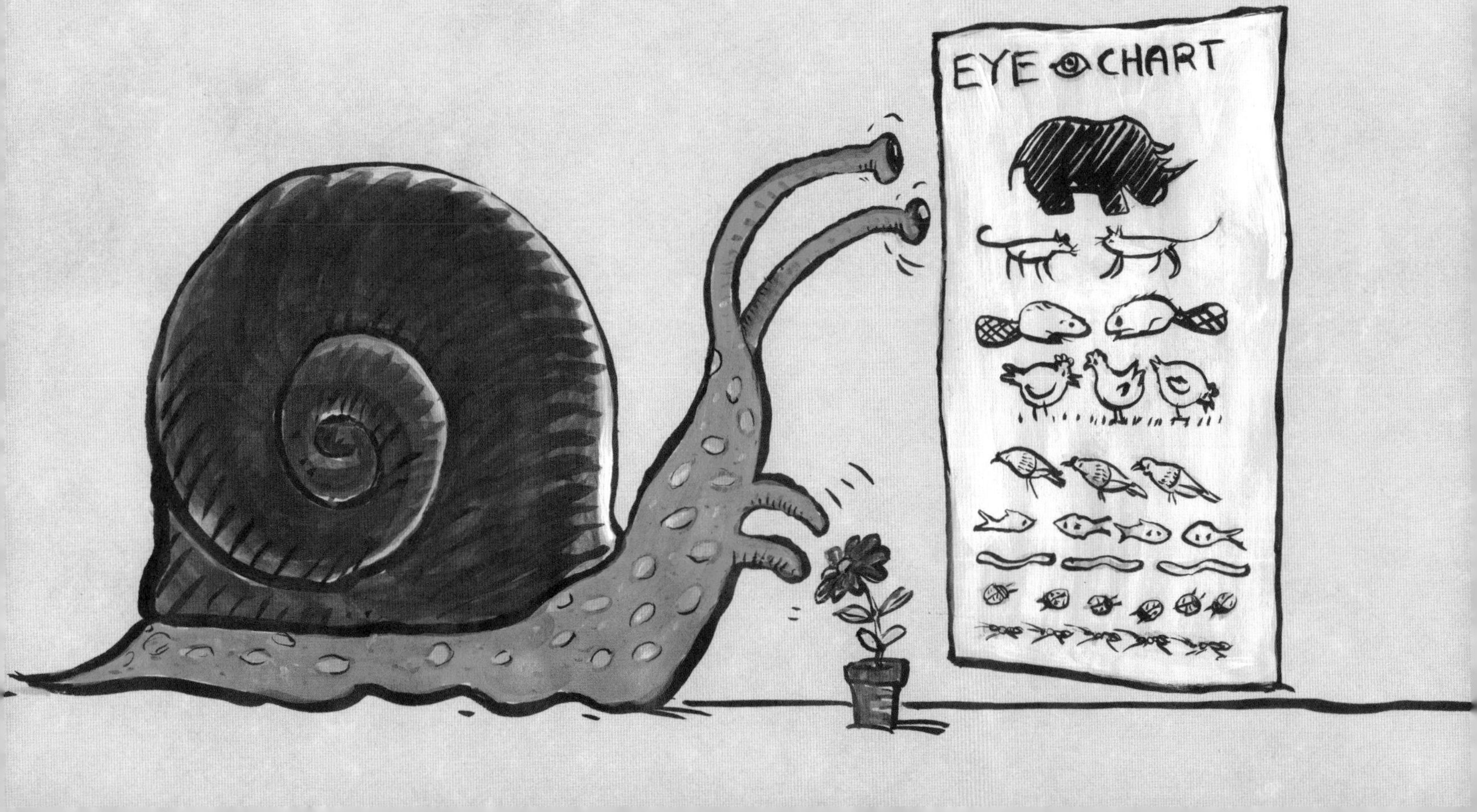
EYE CHART

THERE ARE THOUSANDS OF KINDS OF SNAILS AND MANY MORE TYPES OF SLUGS. SLUGS ARE SNAILS WITHOUT SHELLS.

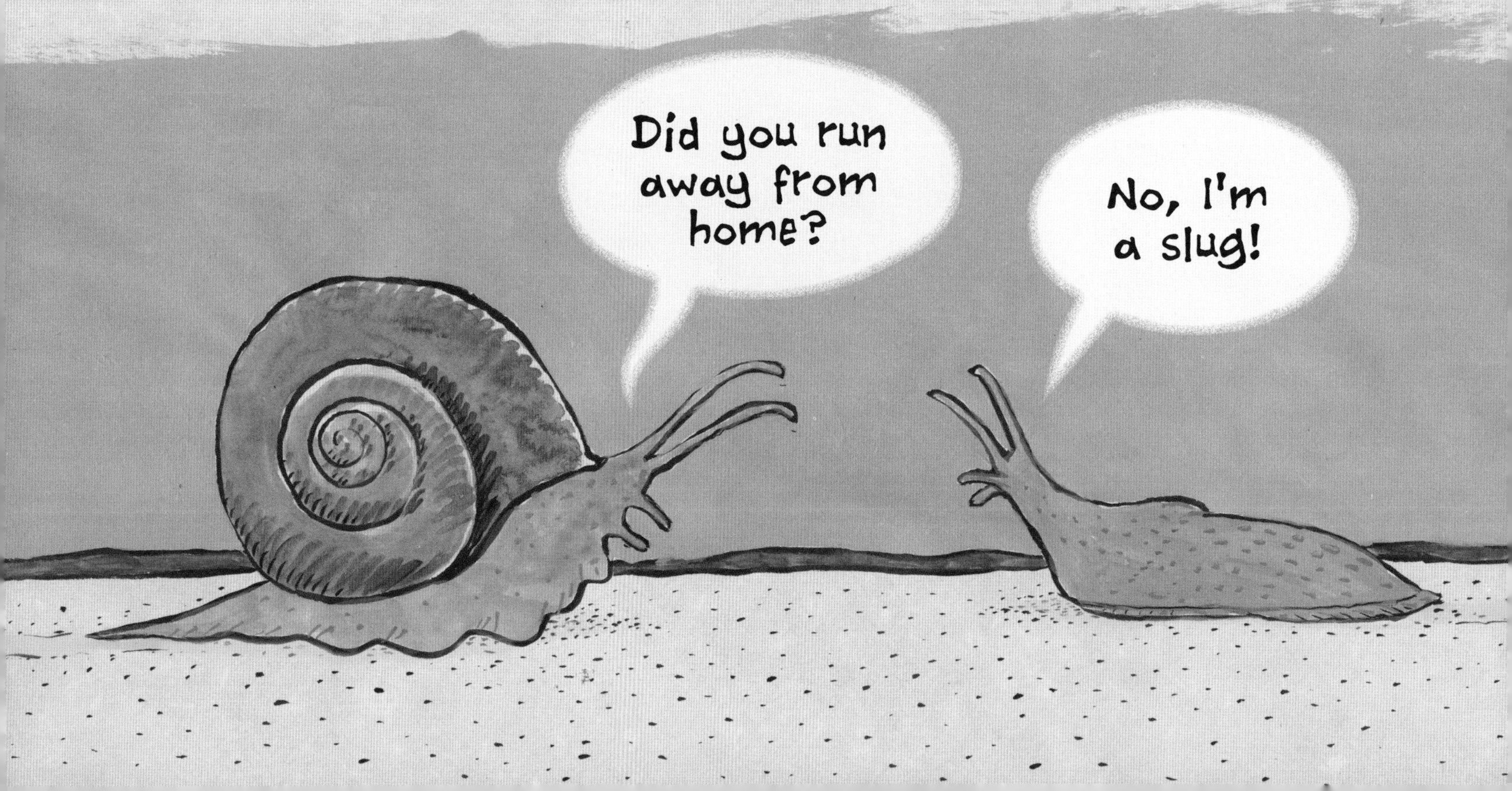
Did you run away from home?
No, I'm a slug!

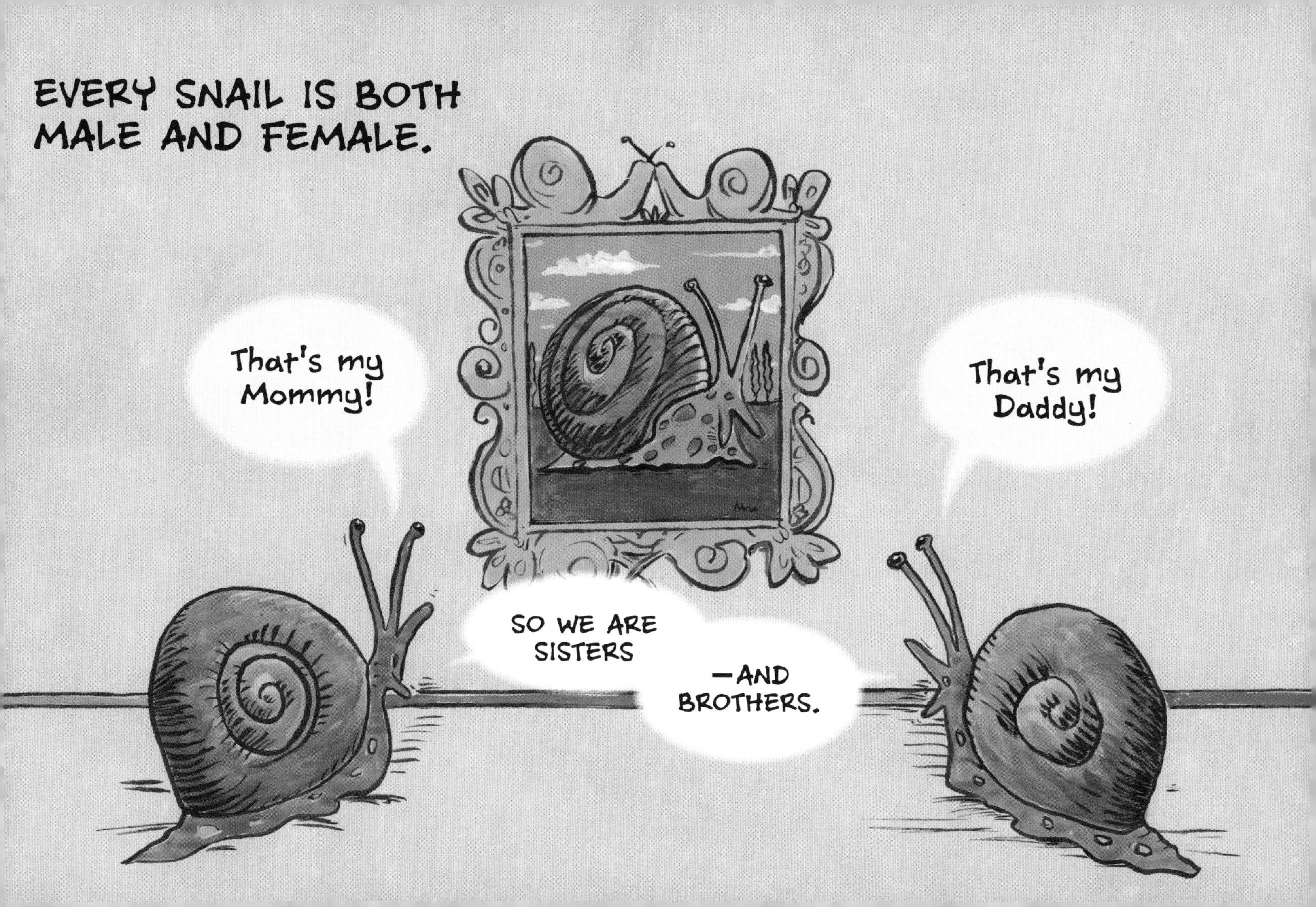
EVERY SNAIL IS BOTH MALE AND FEMALE.
That's my Mommy!
That's my Daddy!
SO WE ARE SISTERS
—AND BROTHERS.

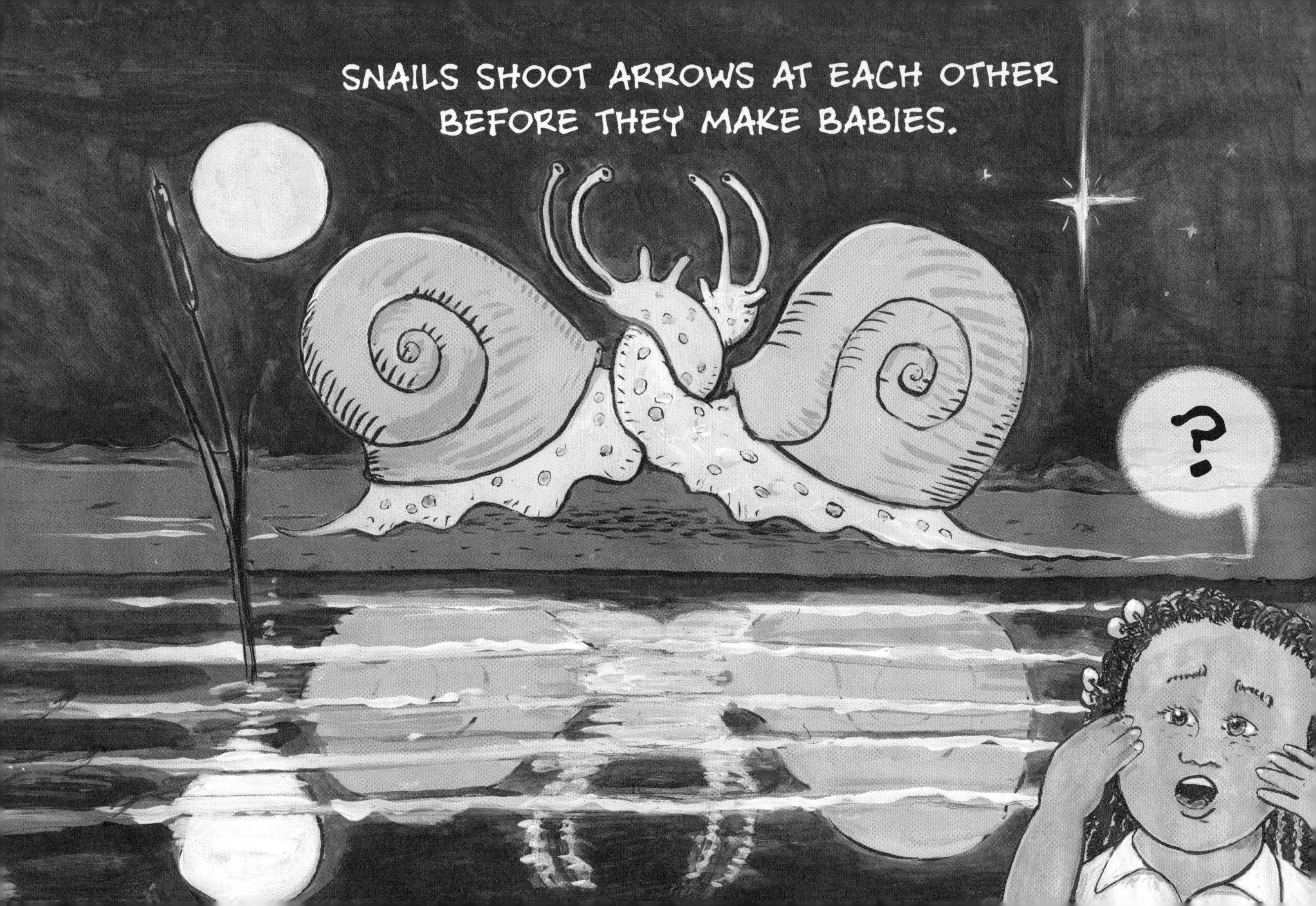
SNAILS SHOOT ARROWS AT EACH OTHER BEFORE THEY MAKE BABIES.
?

THE STORY OF CUPID'S ARROWS MAY HAVE COME FROM SNAILS' "LOVE DARTS."

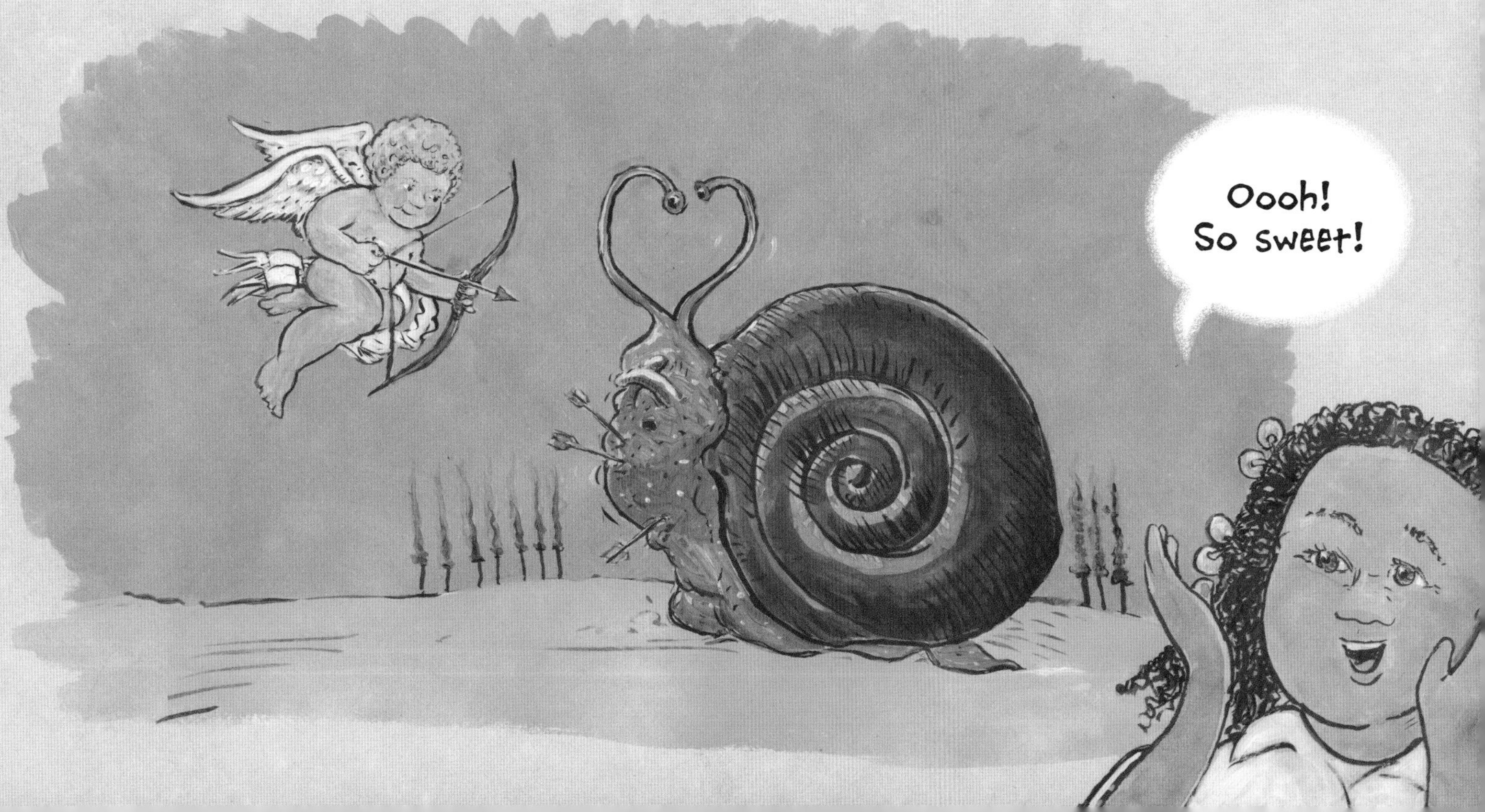
Oooh!
So sweet!

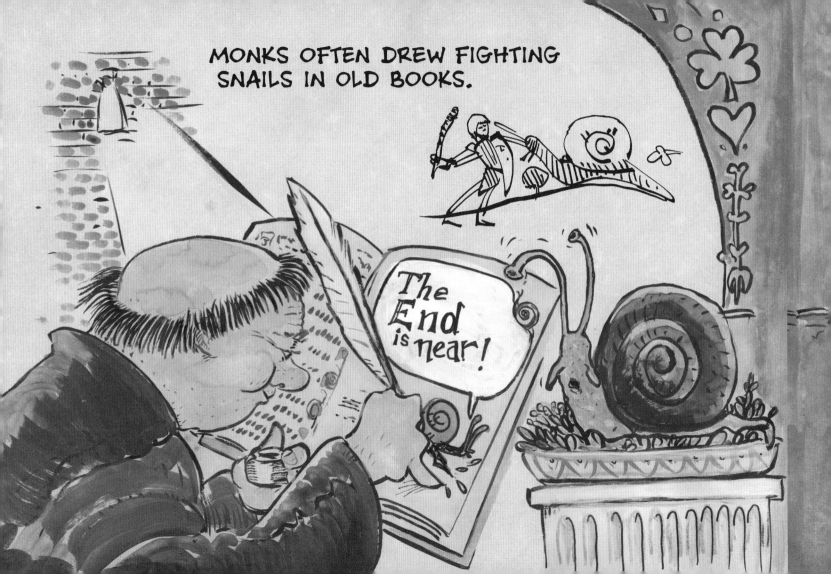

MONKS OFTEN DREW FIGHTING SNAILS IN OLD BOOKS.

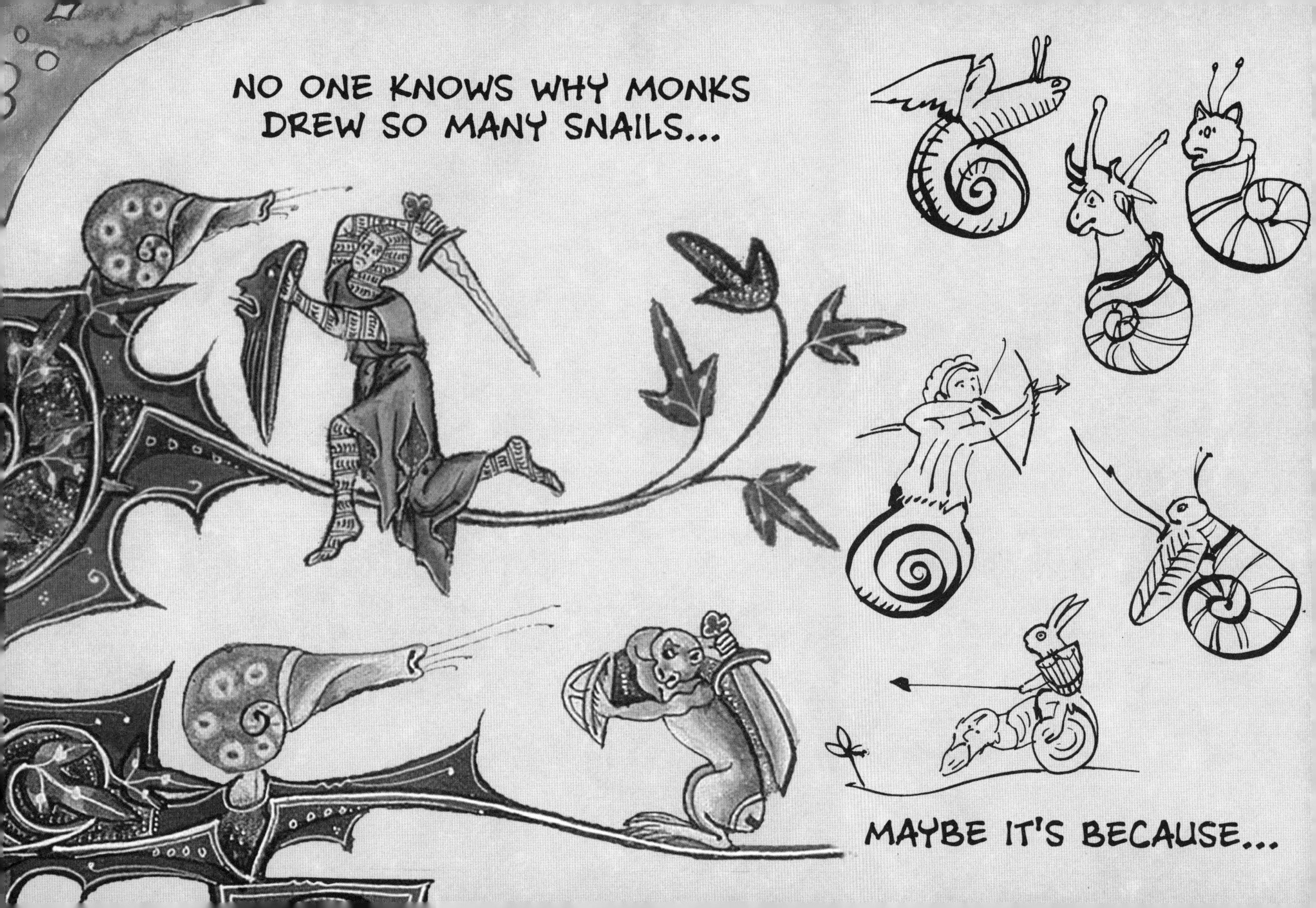
NO ONE KNOWS WHY MONKS DREW SO MANY SNAILS...
MAYBE IT'S BECAUSE...

...SNAILS ARE FUN TO DRAW!

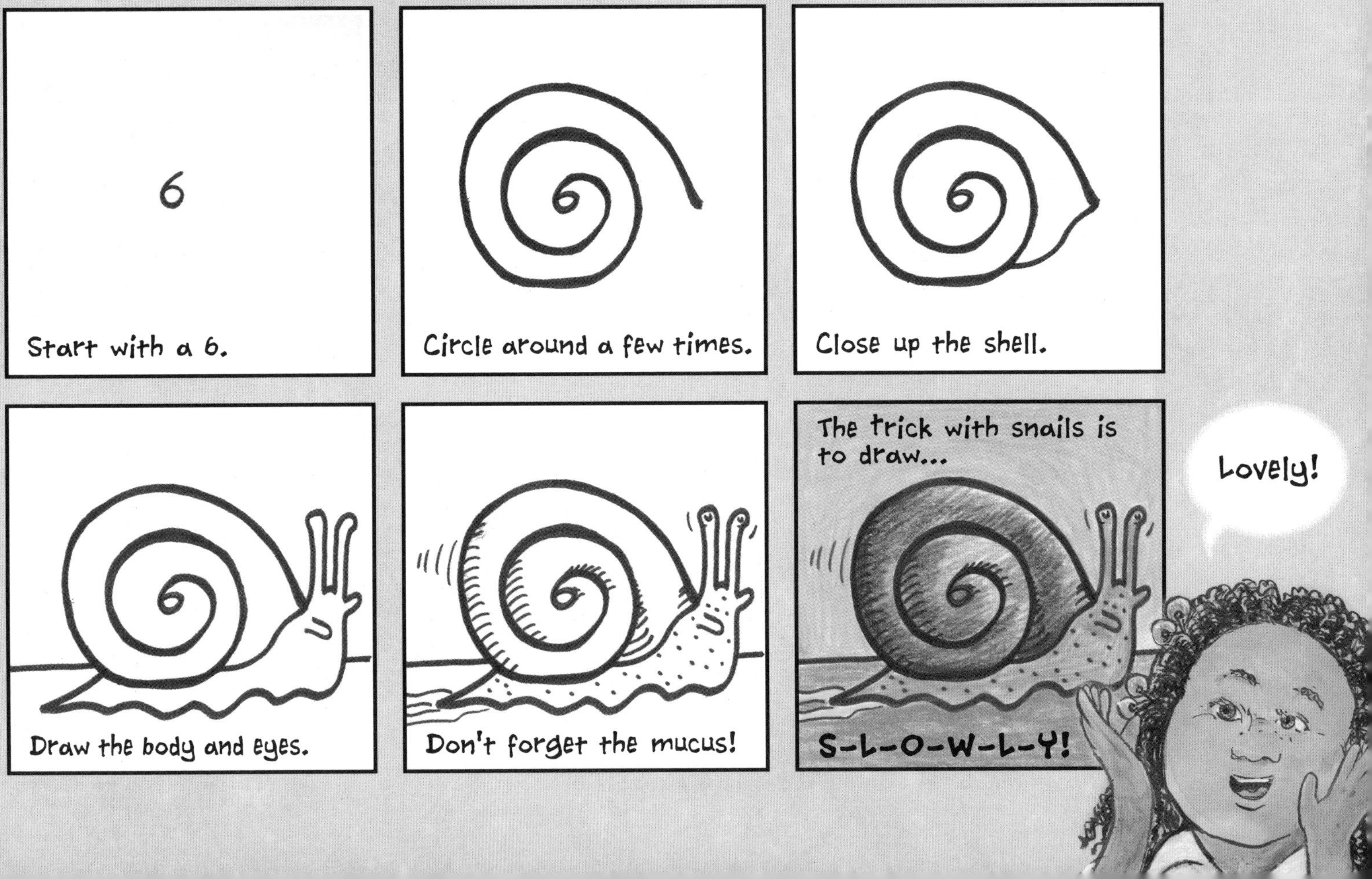
6
Start with a 6.
Circle around a few times.
Close up the shell.
Draw the body and eyes.
Don't forget the mucus!
The trick with snails is to draw...
S-L-O-W-L-Y!
Lovely!

ABOUT THE AUTHOR

KEVIN McCLOSKEY teaches illustration at Pennsylvania's Kutztown University. After writing this book, Kevin is practically a snail expert, but he can't tell us whether the snails served in restaurants are tasty – he's never eaten one. What's the closest he's come to trying snails? Kevin says, "Sometimes, when I cook artichokes, I put a clove of garlic in the leaves. Then when they're cooked, I forget I put the garlic in and I think there's a slug in my food."

HOW TO READ COMICS WITH KIDS

Kids love comics! They are naturally drawn to the details in the pictures, which make them want to read the words. Comics beg for repeated readings and let both emerging and reluctant readers enjoy complex stories with a rich vocabulary. But since comics have their own grammar, here are a few tips for reading them with kids:

GUIDE YOUNG READERS: Use your finger to show your place in the text, but keep it at the bottom of the speaking character so it doesn't hide the very important facial expressions.

HAM IT UP! Think of the comic book story as a play and don't hesitate to read with expression and intonation. Assign parts or get kids to supply the sound effects, a great way to reinforce phonics skills.

LET THEM GUESS. Comics provide lots of context for the words, so emerging readers can make informed guesses. Like jigsaw puzzles, comics ask readers to make connections, so check a young audience's understanding by asking "What's this character thinking?" (but don't be surprised if a kid finds some of the comics' subtle details faster than you).

TALK ABOUT THE PICTURES. Point out how the artist paces the story with pauses (silent panels) or speeded-up action (a burst of short panels). Discuss how the size and shape of the panels carry meaning.

ABOVE ALL, ENJOY! There is of course never one right way to read, so go for the shared pleasure. Once children make the story happen in their imagination, they have discovered the thrill of reading, and you won't be able to stop them. At that point, just go get them more books, and more comics.

www.TOON-BOOKS.com

SEE OUR FREE ONLINE CARTOON MAKERS, LESSON PLANS, AND MUCH MORE